# Shark!

THE CURIOUS NATURALIST SERIES

*Shark!* by R.D. Lawrence
*Birds of Tropical America* by Steven Hilty
*The Wind Birds* by Peter Matthiessen
*Nature's Everyday Mysteries* by Sy Montgomery
*A Natural History of Sex* by Adrian Forsyth

❦

ALSO BY R.D. LAWRENCE

*Wildlife in Canada (1966)*
*The Place in the Forest (1967)*
*Where the Water Lilies Grow (1968)*
*The Poison Makers (1969)*
*Cry Wild (1970)*
*Maple Syrup (1971)*
*Wildlife in North America: Mammals (1974)*
*Wildlife in North America: Birds (1974)*
*Paddy (1977)*
*The North Runner (1979)*
*Secret Go the Wolves (1980)*
*The Study of Life (1980)*
*The Zoo That Never Was (1981)*
*Voyage of the Stella (1982)*
*The Ghost Walker (1983)*
*Canada's National Parks (1983)*
*In Praise of Wolves (1986)*
*Trans Canada Country (1986)*
*The Natural History of Canada (1988)*
*For the Love of Mike (1989)*
*The White Puma (1989)*
*Wolves (1990)*
*Trail of the Wolf (1993)*
*The Green Trees Beyond (1994)*

THE CURIOUS NATURALIST

# Shark!

*Nature's Masterpiece*

By R.D. Lawrence

Illustrated by Gary Low

CHAPTERS™

CHAPTERS PUBLISHING LTD., SHELBURNE, VERMONT 05482

Published by
Chapters Publishing Ltd.
2031 Shelburne Road
Shelburne, Vermont 05482

Trade distribution by
Firefly Books Ltd.
250 Sparks Avenue
Willowdale, Ontario
Canada M2H 2S4

Library of Congress Cataloging-in-Publication Data

Lawrence, R.D., 1921-
    Shark!: nature's masterpiece / by R.D. Lawrence;
illustrations by Gary Low
        p. cm. — (The Curious naturalist)
    Originally published: Toronto: McClelland and Stewart, ©1985.
    Includes index.
    ISBN 1-881527-57-3: $12.95
    1. Sharks. I. Title. II. Series: Curious naturalist series.
    QL638.9.L37 1994
    597'.31 — dc20                                      94-15240

Printed and bound in Canada by
Friesen Printers
Altona, Manitoba

Designed by Hans Teensma/Impress, Inc., Northampton, Massachusetts

Cover painting by Gary Low

# Acknowledgments

I GRATEFULLY acknowledge the assistance given to me in the writing of this book by the following: Dr. James K. Dooley, Associate Professor of Ichthyology, Adelphi University, Garden City, New York; Dr. Samuel H. Gruber, Associate Professor, Division of Biology and Living Resources, University of Miami, Florida; Officials of the National Oceanic and Atmospheric Administration, U.S. Department of Commerce, Narragansett, Rhode Island; Murray A. Palmer, Douro, Ontario, my research assistant; and Dr. John E. Randall, Bishop Museum, Honolulu, Hawaii.

# *Author's Note*

❦

OBSERVED SWIMMING undisturbed in its own world, a shark is a beautiful creature; it is lithe and streamlined and quite without an equal. Wagging the last third of its body from side to side, and in this way displacing water with its large tail fin, a typical shark glides along at a cruising speed of about two miles an hour, its mouth held slightly open, teeth folded inward, out of sight, its staring eyes occasionally showing white rings and its expression benign, even smiling. Each lazy movement of the torpedo-shaped body causes the tight skin to wrinkle and to produce velvety coruscations that alter their colors in accordance with the light that slants into the upper layers of water, which also elicits reflections from the shark's back and flanks. These things, viewed in conjunction with the undersea world, combine to create a silent fantasia that is more powerful and enthralling than the most fanciful musical composition. A single shark traveling in this tranquil state while the tropical sun lances into the ocean is a wonder to behold; a dozen or more similarly at peace offer an observer the ultimate in aesthetic experience.

I formed these conclusions 40 years ago while free diving in the Red Sea, and although I have observed hundreds of sharks of different species during the intervening years, I have not had occasion to change my mind. Indeed, today I hold the sharks in even higher esteem, for I have gotten to know them better, to understand them a little more fully and to admire them a lot. Above all, I respect them, not just because even a small one is quite capable of killing me in the water, but also because sharks are creations that have adapted so wonderfully to their oceanic world that I consider them to be the most physically perfect of all life-forms to be found on land or in the sea.

The majority of observers claim that sharks are unpredictable and therefore more dangerous than any other animal. This is so, they say, because no shark knows what it is going to do next. Such a generalization owes its origin to the fact that no one individual can claim to be a shark expert. At best, those of us who have studied these challenging and mysterious animals have learned to recognize different species by shape, size, color and habitat; we can understand some of a particular shark's traits, and we know a great deal about its anatomy, but we don't know its *mind* and, therefore, we don't know how it is going to react under any one of thousands of given circumstances. For me, such lack of knowledge makes the study of these great fish truly fascinating, for it guarantees that every time I meet a member of the species, I will return to the surface enriched by at least one new piece of information — and inasmuch as there are almost 350 known species of sharks, this means that while I have eyes and a mind with which to reason, the study of these fish will continue to stimulate and intrigue me.

Having become acquainted with sharks when I was too young to have formed prejudices, I viewed them within the context of their environment. They were inhabitants of a world that teemed with other life-forms, and I accepted them as such while realizing that they could be dangerous. But then, I knew from a very early age that the sea itself was dangerous and that it contained many animals that could hurt me if they were molested or handled carelessly. Some of these were only capable of doing minor damage, such as the sea urchins and jellyfish, but the pain they inflicted was severe enough to be avoided; and since these organisms were the first to cause me suffering, they taught me to be cautious of all other life-forms. They also fanned my interest and led me to study them and the many neighbors with which they shared the shallows and shorelines; and soon thereafter, they introduced me to my first shark.

In this way, with the inquisitiveness and wonder of a child, I slowly broadened my knowledge of the sea and eventually graduated to the serious study of sharks. I was cautious but usually unafraid and, without benefit of scholastic or parental instruction, came to realize that it was not possible to understand one organism without also understanding its habitat and the relationships that exist between it and the other living things that use the same environment. From my first awareness of it, the sea became my mentor; it caused me to learn to read at an early age because I wanted to understand the words as well as the pictures I found in my father's many natural history books; it taught me how to count before I was in the first grade because I simply *had* to know how many spines adorned an urchin's shell and how many tentacles were suspended from the body of a jellyfish; and it taught me how to reason. More important, the sea molded my adult life: it turned me into a biologist.

Years later, devoting myself to the study of mammals, the influence of the sea led me to observe the whole environment while concentrating on one particular animal; after that period, I again began to observe sharks. More recently, when following a long absence I returned to the ocean and met an eight-foot blue shark, my lifetime interest in these fish was revived; and although I had no intention of writing about them, I started reading the latest literature dealing with the species.

After poring over a stack of scientific and popular books on sharks, I found myself disappointed in that most authors dealt with these fish in almost total isolation; that is to say, sharks were discussed out of context with their habitat and all the other living things that exist beneath the waters of our seas and oceans. In addition, all the so-called popular books exaggerated the danger sharks posed to humans, in some cases overdramatizing the stories, in others leaving the impression that attacks on humans are increasing at a great rate.

The scientific authors, however, focused on the biology of the shark and some of them described recent interesting experiments that shed new light on the species, but most of these writings are unlikely to gain the attention of lay readers because of their complex style and emphasis on technical language. There are exceptions, of course, the most notable contained in the work of Dr. Eugenie Clark, professor of zoology at the

University of Maryland, and of Dr. Perry Gilbert, of Cornell University. The former wrote a fine article in the August 1981 issue of *National Geographic*, the latter, who has spent many years studying sharks, revealed useful information in a number of reports. In 1975, I found a paperback edition of Dr. H. David Baldridge's *Shark Attack* (Droke House/Hallux, Inc., Anderson, South Carolina: 1974). On the cover of this book the following was printed: *True tales of shark attacks on man — facts more terrifying than the fiction of JAWS*, a device employed to lure readers thirsty for gore. Yet the book is neither fanciful nor exaggerated. It deals exclusively with the Shark Attack File (SAF) started by the U.S. Navy in 1958. Dr. Baldridge, who had done research on shark repellents before going to work on the SAF, studied the available data of shark predation on humans through computer analysis and documented 1,652 cases of shark attack, beginning with the first on record — which took place in 1580 — and bringing the file up to the time of his writing. The book concludes with advice to swimmers and divers and openly states that such advice is formulated on the basis of logic rather than on statistical validity, which is another way of saying that while one particular shark may abandon an attack when the victim does a certain thing, another of the same species may do the reverse.

My search through the available shark writings lasted more than two years, a period during which I even dug into the distant past, researching such observers as Pliny the Elder, the Roman naturalist who referred to the selachians as dogfish — *pescecane*, a name that is used in Italy to this day.

I concluded that a gap existed on the shelves of shark literature; a book was needed that would examine sharks biologically and seek to show their relationship with other marine animals, the relationships that exist between the sharks, their differences, their natural foods and eating habits, the body signals they make while hunting, mating and fighting, and all the other facts that have been discovered over the years but which have been recorded in scattered, unconnected writings. Such a book would also describe the ocean world, much as the land wilderness has already been described. I set out to fill the gap, borrowing heavily from many sources and drawing even more freely on my own long experience with sharks as well as on the many years of research that I have done on dry land, for the creatures of the ocean and the animals of the wilderness are ruled by the same inflexible law of nature, *survival.*

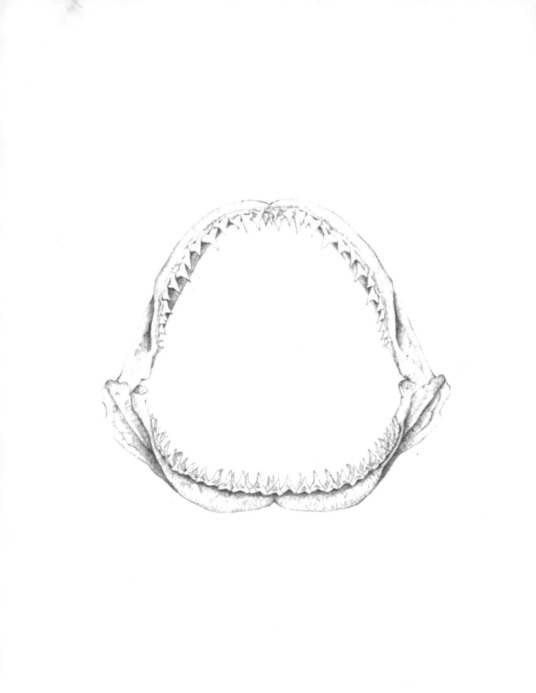

THE JAWS AND TEETH OF A BULL SHARK.
THIS SPECIES CAN GROW TO 10 FEET AND
WEIGH UP TO 500 POUNDS.

# Chapter 1

❧

ON A CLEAR MORNING in July 1930, I sat on a rock shelf some two feet above the water and spent a few minutes looking southward at the placid expanse of the Mediterranean Sea. I was not yet nine years old, my birthday being in September, but I can vividly recall the scene that spread before me and the events that led me to perch on that isolated oceanside rock.

The previous afternoon, diving from the same platform on which I now rested, I had seen a number of young sharks sheltering in the kelp bed that was some 20 feet below the surface, and I had tried in vain to catch one of them with my bare hands during three free dives. The 12-inch predators had been too quick for me, and so I had decided to return in the morning with a fish net, determined to get at least one specimen so that I might keep it alive and study it.

On the way to my aunt's house, where my parents and brother were also staying, I decided to keep my project secret in case parental caution got the upper hand. But I told my brother Jack that I had seen the sharks while diving.

"Boy!" he said. "You're lucky the mother wasn't around or she'd have eaten you!"

Not knowing that shark mothers leave their offspring after they enter the oceanic world, Jack's remark put me in a somber mood and brought to mind the many times I had watched local fishermen unload their catches of assorted, fascinating fish. These often contained at least one shark. I began to visualize those monsters waiting for me in the morning, each displaying its array of viciously serrated teeth after having in some way returned from the dead in order to protect their small relatives.

I was quiet at suppertime; my unusual placidity caused my parents to presume that I was tired, and I was ordered to bed early. Sleep, however, was the last item on my day's agenda. Although I complied with the order by undressing and getting between the sheets, I carried a supply of books dealing with the sea. Two of them contained fanciful stories about sharks. During some spectacular nightmares, I was pulled to pieces and devoured by a succession of gigantic sharks. The last attack must have been truly ferocious because it caused me to wet the bed.

In the morning, shame-faced and nervous, I confessed my night-time lapse to my mother, received a scolding and accepted my punishment. From now on I would not be allowed to drink anything but a glass of warm milk at suppertime. However, the deprivation of my usual glass of watered-down wine — which I infinitely preferred to warm milk — caused me no anguish. My mind full of sharks, I ate breakfast without appetite and waited impatiently for a full hour to elapse before seeking permission to "go out and play," knowing that my parents believed it was dangerous to go swimming right after a meal.

During the interval, I sat under the almond trees on the terrace, still determined to capture a shark but feeling apprehensive about diving into the kelp bed. Until that point in time, there had been many things that had made me fearful, but the sea had never been one of them. I had always loved the water, perhaps because my association with it had begun before and during my birth, when the turbulence of the Atlantic Ocean had caused my mother to enter into labor while the vessel in which my family travelled was still making for land. Such a supposition is, of course, greatly aided by hindsight, but whatever the reason, it is a fact that when my father carried me into the waters of the Atlantic during my first summer of life, I became delighted until I was taken back to the beach. Then, I am told, I screamed my small head off and would not be quiet until I was once more dunked in the ocean.

I have no memory of those events, but I do recall the first time I managed to swim unaided. I was three years old; my family was vacationing on the shores of the Costa Brava, a Mediterranean Sea resort not far from the city of Barcelona, Spain, where I grew up after we had moved there from Vigo, which is on the Atlantic coast.

Before my fourth summer, I had been taken into the sea often by my parents or my brothers, but in July 1925, while I was still somewhat awkward on land, I walked into the water on my own accord, advancing until I disappeared from sight. My mother, who later said she had not seen me enter the sea, looked for me at the moment when my head was going under. I am told she had a fit. Her distress was premature, however, for my head reappeared and I was observed "dog-paddling" away from land. Father dashed to rescue me, a small boy who was reported to be loudly opposed to salvation.

Before the end of that summer, I had even learned to dive, a circumstance brought about by the fact that my brother Jack, who was six years my senior, took to splashing me whenever my parents weren't watching. Seeking to escape, I ducked under the water and found it was easier to swim beneath the surface than on top of it. Now, secure from my brother's teasing, the buoyancy and freedom I discovered in that sun-dappled submarine world filled me with delight. Insulated from the adults and elder siblings, my self-confidence grew as, with eyes opened wide, I began to observe and collect bottom organisms at depths of six or seven feet.

In this way, I found personal independence at a very early age. As the youngest in the family, I had hitherto had to rely on my parents, brothers and sister for entertainment and assistance; but now I could manage on my own, to the point where I resented when others interfered with my activities. Two years later, I had become a proficient diver; and although my surface style was inelegant, I was a strong swimmer.

When I was six, my Aunt Nita, Father's older sister, bought a villa in Palma de Mallorca, the capital city of Spain's Balearic islands that lie almost equidistant between the coast of Barcelona and the shores of Algeria, and from that time on, Jack and I summered there, our parents accompanying us and staying for two weeks before returning to the mainland — an overnight boat trip — and leaving us in the care of our devoted and fascinating aunt. She was at that period retired from a long career of nursing and had been the matron of a military hospital in South Africa during the Boer War.

Aunt Nita kept us spellbound with accounts of that turn-of-the-century conflict. My favorite, which I demanded again and again, concerned a Major Sturton whom my aunt had nursed after his left foot was bitten off by a shark. The major had been swimming in the Indian Ocean, off the Durban coast, and was a mile from land when the predatory fish struck. Apart from the loss of his foot, 209 stitches were needed to close the wounds on his legs and back. Since I had once required three stitches when I had dived too steeply and hit bottom with my head, I remember trying to decide which agony would have been greater for the major: that inflicted by the teeth of the shark, or the one produced by the needle and thread wielded by the doctor!

My aunt's villa was located in the district of El Terreno, just outside Palma. From the front terrace, the wide, deep bay fronting the island's biggest city was visible. The Mediterranean, always deep blue on clear days, stretched southward as far as the eye could see, an azure expanse that spelled adventure to a small boy who had become bewitched by the sea. Behind the house was a high stone wall that furnished a surmountable barrier between the villa and the Bellver Forest, a great expanse of pine woods surrounding a medieval Moorish castle that attracted me almost as much as the nearby ocean. North of the forest, in terraced rows made necessary by the steep terrain, stood groves of orange trees, their fruits bright and sunny, their shiny, smooth leaves deep green. On land that was too precipitous for farming grew clumps of carob trees, their long, beanlike seedpods ripened and turned purply black. In other places grew clumps of prickly-pear cactus and solitary agaves, or sisal yuccas, plants with stiff, pulpy leaves that were edged with sharp spines and tipped by a hard black spike. Great, gnarled olive trees, some of them said to be more than a thousand years old, grew in ragged lines on some of the gentler slopes.

Recollections of the forest and the sea, of the oranges and olives and cacti, and of the blazing sun and the dancing haze it generated are still easy to evoke. But I do not need to rely on memory to experience again the emotional contradictions that I struggled with on the morning when I was to catch my first shark. My desire to capture a shark was so strong that I was ready to encounter a fearful situation.

After breakfast, I collected the net, coaxed a sandwich from my mother and wrapped it in oilcloth and left the house, promising to be back in good time for supper.

I was dressed only in shorts, under which I wore my swim trunks, and my feet were encased in rope-soled canvas shoes, or *alpargatas,* as they are called in Spanish, that I usually kept on when swimming because of the many sea urchins inhabiting the bottom. I also had an empty canvas shopping bag in which I could carry marine specimens that had to remain in water until liberated into one of the rock pools I used as aquariums.

Although there were beaches within a five-minute walk of my aunt's villa, my favorite place was two miles away, a secluded area of rocky coast with only a few small beaches. Walking along the highway that led from Palma to Cas Catala, a small fishing village some miles away, I remember the sun was so hot that it melted the tar on the road. It stuck to the soles of my shoes, causing me to take to the shoreline rocks, thus slowing my progress and giving me more time to think of the mother sharks that I was sure would be lurking near the kelp bed.

I suppose I spent about an hour walking and thinking before I arrived at the small beach from where, about 150 yards from shore, a tall, bare rock island shaped like a sugarloaf rose abruptly. I had found the place the previous summer and had made it my own. The shelf that faced seaward was about eight feet long by four feet wide, a smooth platform backed by craggy, crevice-full granite into which I secreted those odds and ends that small boys cherish, things like fishhooks and line, a bamboo pole I had fixed up as a rod, tins for bait and other treasures that had to be kept hidden from prying eyes. Below the shelf was a cave, the entrance to which was under the surface. The roof of this grotto rose above the level of the highest tide, and a long, angling crack continued upward through the granite to show a tiny frame of light at the place where it emerged at the highest point of the sugarloaf. This was my most secret place, a bolt hole into which I could swim whenever the need for solitude seized me. Here, too, I had hiding places, shelves and crannies where I could store my most precious possessions.

The kelp bed was located near the entrance to the cave, and it had been while swimming out of the grotto on a previous day that I beheld my first shark.

Before I reached the water that morning, I took off my shorts, emptied the pockets into the canvas "specimen bag," then hid the garment within a clump of broom. I entered the sea and began swimming for my island, my pace faster than usual and my emotions keyed to high pitch in expectation of a shark attack. Climbing out of the water on the landward side of the rocky island, I scrambled over the top and descended to the shelf, where I sat looking out to sea while trying to find the courage to put my plan into action.

The water between me and the horizon was placid, its waves small and smooth, glassine corrugations that traveled shoreward so gently that they hardly made noise as they spent themselves against the rocks. Gulls flitted gracefully against the blue sky and fish jumped occasionally. Below me, the sea was translucent, so clear that I could see every detail of the bottom, which was composed of a mixture of sand and fallen rock. Several dozen sea urchins were feeding on algae or on small, dead fish, now and then "walking" very slowly by pulling with their forward, lower spines and pushing with their backward spikes. Moving swiftly along the bottom, or swimming above it, a variety of small to medium-sized fish kept busy, some of them ingesting things that were not visible to me, others chasing their fellows, intent on making a kill. Farther away, to the right, I could see the kelp bed, its ribbonlike leaves moving with the current, an occasional red mullet about ten inches long showing itself briefly as it hunted or skulked.

As I looked into the crystalline water, my interest grew and my apprehension receded. I stood up, keeping my gaze fixed on the sea; then, holding the net in one hand, I jumped into the water, electing to enter it in this way because I knew that the handle of the net would have got in the way of a dive. As the sea closed over my head, I turned to a horizontal position, kicking with my feet and sculling with my left arm, going down until I was within a yard of the kelp. I thrust the net handle into the waistband of my trunks, pushing it through until it lay alongside my left thigh.

With both hands free, I approached the kelp, reaching outward to part the green fronds, feeling no apprehension as I savored the freedom offered by the buoyant seawater. Moving slowly, I advanced, my arms entering first, then, as my head was thrust into the slippery forest of fronds and my vision restricted to only a few inches ahead, I backed out, realizing I could not hope to spot a shark while engulfed by the kelp. Instead, I swam around the bed, keeping one arm in it so as to create a disturbance, but I had not reached the halfway point when my need for oxygen drove me back to the surface.

As I turned and started to rise, I caught sight of the three small sharks. One after the other they shot out of the kelp, curved around the outside fronds and darted back into concealment. Exhaling as I went up, I broke the surface, sucked air in deeply and dived, making for the place where I had dropped the net. Again I was frustrated in my attempts to catch a shark. I repeated the performance again and yet again.

In this way, I continued to dive and to miss my targets. Now that their hiding place was continuously being disturbed, the sharks darted about constantly, allowing me to see them during almost every descent; but by lunchtime, when I was too cold to dive anymore, I was as far away from fulfilling my objective as I had been the previous day.

Lying in the broiling sun for ten minutes soon put heat back into my body. I ate my sandwich and immediately became thirsty, but since I had not brought drinking water with me, I went back into the sea, feeling only slightly guilty because I was disobeying my parents by swimming so soon after eating.

During this dive, I changed tactics. Instead of swimming outside the bed, I went through it, struggling somewhat to force a passage because the floating, snaky fronds clung to me and occasionally caused me to kick hard when my ankles became entangled in the strong leaves. When I came out at the other side, a distance of about 50 feet from where I entered, I was delighted to see seven sharklets milling about just beneath me. I took a quick swipe with the net, missed, then had to rise for air.

Moments later I was down again, repeating the same maneuver, and this time, perhaps because I expected to see the sharks, I was ready with the net in my right hand when I came out of the kelp. Just as before, the sharks were right beneath me; five of them now. Waving my left arm wildly as I brought down the net, I managed to stampede one of the fish. It blundered into the net. I grabbed it, having no difficulty holding its body because of the sandpaperlike quality of shark skin. Up I went with my captive, and although I had a little trouble climbing onto my rock shelf one-handed, I managed it and was at last able to examine the shark. It appeared to be somewhat smaller than the others, being about ten inches long. Wrapping it in the mesh of the net to prevent it from escaping, I put it down while I dipped the canvas bag in the sea and filled it with water. The bag leaked, but the rate of escape was slow and I was confident I could keep refilling the container from the nearby shore while I walked the two miles back home. First, however, I had to close the mouth of the bag and swim to the beach with my prize, not the easiest thing for a nine-year-old to do while carrying a container weighted by about two gallons of sea.

It was midafternoon when I arrived at my aunt's house, disheveled and out of breath and clad only in my swim trunks because I had completely forgotten to retrieve my shorts. Yet my timing was right, for my parents had gone out, my brother was off somewhere on his own and Aunt Nita was in the kitchen. Rummaging in the garden shed until I found an old pail, I dashed away, filled the bucket with fresh seawater and put the now rather limp shark into it. For an hour after that I sat over the pail, watching the fish anxiously, occasionally putting my hand underneath it when it appeared to be sinking to the bottom.

I was still gazing solicitously at my captive when my parents re-turned, neither one noticing me as I squatted in the garden; but as the shark began to swim awkwardly in its confining prison, I picked up the pail and went inside to show off my prize. My mother saw it first and immediately banished me and my "pet" from the house, reminding me that I wasn't supposed to introduce fish into my aunt's home. Trying to coax Mother into making an exception in this case, I explained that the pail's occupant wasn't really a fish but a shark.

Mother had evidently failed to realize that the creature in the bucket was a member of the selachian family, but now she became quite agitated, ordering me to take the "nasty beast" and throw it back in the sea or, better still, kill it.

In the middle of the ensuing argument, my father entered the living room and, on learning the facts, immediately came to my side. He saw no reason why I should not be allowed to keep the shark outside the house. It was, after all, he explained to my mother, small and harmless and would almost certainly die of its own accord in the not too distant future. Mother became mollified, and as she insisted that it be taken out of the house immediately, my father lowered an exploratory index finger into the bucket, evidently intending to poke its occupant. Eager to cement our unexpected alliance, I tipped the pail slightly, allowing the shark to straighten its tail just as my father's finger entered the water.

Without any warning, the shark straightened and moved forward at remarkable speed, its small mouth open wide. In a trice, the tiny but razor-sharp teeth closed on the tip of my father's finger. The shark bit hard and started to swing its head from side to side, causing the blood to flow. My father yelled and withdrew his hand from the bucket, elevating the shark at the same time. But far from releasing its hold, the shark bit deeper, and my father, yelling more loudly, shook his hand vigorously.

The shark was dislodged, but as its teeth were forced along the fingertips, my father's skin was seriously lacerated. As I tried to retrieve the agitated fish from under a chair, where it was wriggling and lashing with its tail while snapping its small jaws, my aunt came rushing into the living room. Further commotion ensued, but I was too occupied with my own affairs to pay much attention to the fuss. Having seen what the shark could do with its baby teeth, I developed a sudden, healthy respect for it, and so I became cautious when I finally closed my hand over its body at a point between its dorsal fin and tail. As I lifted the fish, it swung its head, mouth agape, and tried to bite my hand, but I managed to put it back in the bucket without injury before retreating to the garden.

Now I was sure that my shark was going to be killed, so I decided to look at it for as long as possible prior to its demise. While I was doing so, I listened to the heightened voices emerging from the house. My father was furious over "that confounded fish!" My aunt, clearly exercising her profession, was telling him not to keep moving his hand. And my mother was laughing. That was curious! I couldn't help rising and approaching the house and I was just in time to hear my mother say to my father that his injury was deserved. Then she laughed again and added that if he hadn't stuck his finger in the shark's mouth, it wouldn't have bitten him. It seemed that Mother had switched sides and was now championing my cause.

In the end, because my father had a good sense of humor, he saw the funny side of the incident and I was allowed to build a seaside pen for the shark, where it lived for a week without eating, then died. Using a sharp pocket knife, I dissected it, examining those of its organs that were not mangled by my unskilled cutting.

In retrospect, I cannot be sure of the species to which my first shark belonged, but I believe it may have been a brown or sandbar shark (*Carcharhinus milberti*), a species not uncommon in the Mediterranean. The second specimen I obtained that year was a cat shark (*Scyliorhinus stellaris*), known in Britain as the greater-spotted dogfish. This species lays a single egg that is protected by a leathery case equipped with tendrils at each end; these ribbons become entangled in marine plants and serve to anchor the egg case until the embryo reaches maturity. Because they are used as food in many parts of Europe, I was familiar with the species, having seen them among the catches of the local fishermen. The individual that came into my possession, a female almost three feet long, did so of her own accord when she took a bait I had been dangling in the water in the hope of catching a red mullet, or goatfish.

On this occasion, I had been fishing offshore rocks in an area where the depth was about 40 feet, but because the water was so clear, I could see the bottom and the fish that lurked down there. Two mullets had darted to inspect the piece of squid I had affixed to the hook, but each fish had rejected the food. I had been about to reel the line in and change the bait when the shark came, swimming lazily and only inches from the bottom. Without hesitation, the sinuous, spotted fish opened its mouth and bit the squid, shaking its head from side to side when it felt resistance. It virtually hooked itself without realizing that it had done so, for it turned casually and tried to swim away. Only then did it react, charging left and right while shaking the front half of its body, stirring up a cloud of sand from the bottom.

I started to reel in line and was surprised by the ease with which the shark came up. A conventional fish of that size would have struggled violently, causing the bamboo rod to bend into a hoop, but the shark seemed to be following the pull of the line, its struggles ceasing as soon as it came off the bottom. Peace ended when the first of the two dorsal fins broke the surface. Now it seemed that the shark had become aware that it was in trouble. It turned, trying to go down, then it swung left, ran some distance despite my resistance, shot upward, turned right for another run, tried to dive once more. Rising again, it stopped fighting as suddenly as it had started, maintaining itself afloat, both fins showing above the water and mouth open to reveal vicious-looking teeth.

My line was not designed for such a fish, having only about a six-pound breaking stress, so I was in somewhat of a quandary as to what to do with the shark now that it was more or less subdued and ready to be taken out of the water. If I tried to lift it out by rod and line, I was sure it would struggle and break free, yet I couldn't ease it ashore because of the rocks that rose two feet above the water.

Writing about the incident in hindsight, I can be calm enough, but at the time I wanted that shark desperately and I was ready to do anything to find it a home in a deep tide pool, where I could watch it to my heart's desire.

I solved my difficulty by wrapping some line around my left hand and cutting the rest free from the rod before going into the water, which reached up to my chest at shoreline. The cat shark didn't react to my entry into its world. It continued to swim slowly, staying at surface level and tugging occasionally as though to make sure that it was still tethered. I walked toward it, winding loose line around my hand at first. When only about four feet separated us, the water up to my neck, I began pulling the fish toward me, working slowly so as to cause the least disturbance.

The cat shark family comprises a number of species that are usually found in temperate waters. They are considered the most primitive of all sharks and are easily distinguished by the fact that the majority of them have two dorsal fins, the first of which originates well behind the pectoral fins. In addition, the tail does not point upward, running instead on a horizontal line with the body. One species, the brown cat shark (*Apristurus brunneus*), which grows to a length of three feet, is found off the west coast of North America, from California to the straits of Georgia at least as far north as Nanaimo, on the east side of Vancouver Island. The particular species that occupied me that far-off day was decorated by large, dark roundish spots, some of them two or three inches in diameter, others mere dots. Because the first dorsal fin was so far back — it was located immediately above the pelvic fin — the fish had a rather sinister appearance, snakelike, giving the illusion of greater length. Its eyes, as cold and staring as those of all sharks, were relatively large, the pupils mere slits that ran vertically rather than horizontally.

Looking into those eyes, I couldn't help remembering the injury that the ten-inch shark had inflicted on my father's finger. Unlike the eyes of most sharks, which are round, those of the cat-shark are almond-shaped, giving my captive a more human appearance that seemed to increase its sinister countenance. The water was now almost up to my chin. The shark was about 18 inches in front of my face, its mouth open; its pearly, sharp teeth, though not elevated and ready to bite, were clearly visible, leaning inward and reflecting the light, which was also glinting on the hook shank and on the now mangled piece of squid that peeped out of the corner of the predatory mouth.

I remember feeling afraid, but I was also fascinated and more determined than ever to take possession of that fish. As I reached forward slowly, with both hands, the cat shark turned on its side and I thought it was going to dive. This made me grab for it and my hands closed on its body as it was moving. The result was that when I raised it over my head, gripping as tightly as I could manage, the fish was in an upside-down position. To my amazement, it lay passive! I had expected a good struggle as I waded toward shore, but the shark remained absolutely quiet.

Reaching the rocks, I tossed my prize ashore and scrambled after it. The unfortunate fish was now dancing madly, curving its body and lashing its tail and snapping its jaws in an attempt to get back into its natural element. I stopped, timed my movements and grabbed it around the body, my right hand holding it just behind the pectoral fins and my left gripping the tail.

The shark was lifted right-way up and it immediately fought strongly, jerking its body convulsively and turning its head, definitely trying to bite. On the spur of the moment I turned it upside down again, a reflexive action motivated more by hope than reason: it had remained docile while being carried upside down, it might again be induced to become quiet if carried the same way.

To my relief and surprise, the shark immediately relaxed. Eyes staring, mouth slightly agape, it remained as though in a trance as I carried it to a deep, large rock pool that was connected to the sea during high tide. Here I had gathered a number of other specimens of marine life, including three octopuses, an assortment of fish and a number of large crabs, all of which now complemented the natural population of the pool.

The sea penetrated the surface of this small lagoon at only one place, a depressed part of the seaward rocks that was about a foot below the high-tide line. This lip was four feet wide and I found that, by building a wall with small boulders, the water could still enter the pool by seeping through the interstices that remained between the rocks, but the organisms I put in could not escape to sea. It was a natural aquarium, approximately 40 feet long by as many wide, somewhat rounded and about 20 feet deep. Ten feet down, on the seaward side, there were a number of cracks in the rock wall that also allowed water to enter and leave, but they were so narrow that only small organisms could squeeze through.

Here I put the cat shark. Although it earned a living by eating a number of its fellow captives as well as more than a few of the local residents, I augmented its rations with pieces of squid and coarse fish I obtained free from the local fishing boats, whose crews had befriended me because of my interest in their doings and also because I would often do small favors for them.

I especially liked to gut the sharks they brought in, a job that none of them cared for because the intestinal cavity of a shark, even a very fresh one, produces a strong, unpleasant odor, an ammoniac, offallike stench. It should not be supposed that I enjoyed either the smell or the slimy results of the job, but my interest in sharks and fish was stronger than any feelings of revulsion I may have had. And, of course, I obtained a lot of bait in this way, for it was rare that a shark stomach was empty of all but entrails and liver. Most of them had at least one fish inside, and sometimes strange objects were my reward for the job, things like cups and cans. Once I found a hammer with a broken handle. From one big shark — at seven feet, it was big to me — I obtained a balled-up piece of fishing net that, when spread out, was about 10 feet long and 15 wide. The cord was still in good condition where it had not been chewed by the shark's teeth, and I was able to salvage quite a lot of it, which I later used to capture new specimens for my tide pool.

I also collected shark teeth and eyes. By the time I was 12 years old, I had half a dozen glass jars filled with selachian eyes, preserved in formalin, supplies I purchased with my never plentiful pocket money.

The cat shark, being larger and in better condition than my first specimen, thrived in the pool and became so accustomed to me that, before the summer ended, it would come and take food from my hand. Although it would not allow itself to be held, it didn't object to gentle rubbing, which was something I enjoyed doing because of the feel of its rough skin.

When it was time to return to the mainland and to school, I removed the barricade I had made, leaving the denizens of the pool to stay or to go, according to their inclinations. Some, including the cat shark and a two-foot-long octopus, remained, a fact that I discovered the following summer.

Between my first encounter with the small sharks at the age of eight and my last meeting with a Mediterranean shark when I was thirteen, I collected a total of 23 selachians. About half of these died in captivity because I did not know how to care for them, but the others lived until they escaped or were released.

When opportunity presented itself, I also collected barracuda, the largest of which was one meter in length. This specimen was not allowed to remain in the pool for long because it devoured anything within reach of its great fang-filled jaws. It was incredibly fast and a voracious feeder that tackled anything its size or smaller. What amazed me then was that the barracuda ate so much and the sharks ate so little. Having been brought up on stories that stressed the voracious appetite of sharks, I had expected my captives to keep me busy furnishing food for them. Instead, I discovered that sharks, though capable of frantic behavior when they are extremely hungry or excited by competition from others of their kind, were actually quite fussy eaters that, pound for pound, consumed less food than conventional fishes half their size. At the time, I assumed that captivity was affecting their eating habits; later, I was to learn differently.

My final contact with a shark in Palma de Mallorca occurred in August of 1935, a few days before my return to the mainland. Our encounter was accidental and I would have avoided it if I had been given the opportunity to do so, because the shark was at least seven feet long.

My aunt had been called to nurse an English tourist who was burned to a crisp while sunbathing, and as a result we were staying at the Hotel Mediterraneo, where the patient was vacationing. Although the hotel was beside the sea and had a good beach, I didn't care for the crowds, preferring solitary shorelines. But there was one feature of the Mediterraneo that I liked. This was a sort of tower that had been built into the sea, a structure connected to one of the hotel terraces by a tiled walkway. A number of outdoor tables were set so that tourists could enjoy a drink or a meal while sitting 25 feet above the water. The turreted platform was ringed by a wrought-iron fence that was waist-high, and I enjoyed climbing over the fence and diving from there, entering the water at a steep angle and being taken right down to the bottom by the momentum of the dive. Since the turret was some distance from the beach, I could explore the bottom undisturbed by the commotion made by noisy swimmers.

With this in mind, I climbed over the fence, positioned my feet on the narrow outside ledge and got ready to go down. It was not possible to make a running dive, so I had developed a technique whereby, as my body passed beyond the point of balance, I would kick slightly against the cement and thus attain enough forward momentum to clear the buttress below, which was wider at the bottom than at the top. Just as I had become overbalanced and there was no possibility of recovery, I looked down and saw the shark. There wasn't much time to inspect the big fish, but it appeared to be swimming very slowly.

Going down with my eyes wide open, seeing that shark right underneath me, caused me to panic. When I entered the water, instead of gradually checking my descent, I suddenly turned my open hands upward. As a result, my body whiplashed violently and I must have come within an ace of breaking my back. The pain was so acute that I forgot about the shark.

On the surface, some 75 yards from shore and completely alone, I found myself only able to scull with my arms and incapable of using my legs. As I moved awkwardly through the water, I remembered the shark and knew that erratic, noisy movements such as I was making were likely to attract the predator. But my only chance of survival was to get ashore quickly; otherwise, I would drown. To resort to the vernacular, I had placed myself between a rock and a hard place! Below me, I was sure, lurked a big shark; ahead of me lay about 200 feet of deep water. My back hurt like a giant toothache and I was afraid my legs were paralyzed.

I made it to shore and was incapacitated for two weeks by some torn muscles. I learned the futility of giving way to panic. That shark, I am sure, headed for the deeps as soon as it felt the violent and unexpected splash created when my body hit the water.

That was to be my last childhood experience with a shark. In July 1936, civil war broke out in Spain and I became otherwise engaged. But five years later, during the turmoil of World War II, I managed to engineer a few opportunities to again study selachians, this time "graduating" to larger specimens while diving in the Red Sea.

THE BLACK-TIPPED SHARK,
WHICH GROWS TO 9 FEET ANDS WEIGHS UP TO
375 POUNDS, IS KNOWN TO HAVE ATTACKED
EIGHT HUMANS TO DATE.

# Chapter 2

❧

BOUNDED ON the east by Israel and on the west by Egypt, the Sinai Peninsula is shaped somewhat like a stone arrowhead, its point thrusting into the Red Sea between the Gulf of Aqaba and the Gulf of the Suez. At the southernmost tip of this arid and furnace-hot land, a sharp promontory extends into the water and forms a natural well-protected bay called Ras Muhammad. Here, on the morning of July 16, 1941, I stood with a friend in company of a bearded Arab fisherman whose rather slovenly felucca lay offshore, its lateen sails furled and its narrow-waisted shape bobbed on the gentle swell. In the distance, a destroyer of the Royal Navy was steaming south on war patrol; behind us, upslope, a young Bedu boy sat on a boulder, clutching a tubular flute, impervious to the fierce heat as he watched a small herd of black goats in his charge.

Brahim Abdullah, owner-captain of the becalmed boat, was a grizzled man of about 50, a sailor since boyhood who was known to be an expert shark fisherman; and it was for this reason that we had expressed interest in chartering his boat for a week. As we stood barefooted in the water to get relief from the hot, pumicelike sand, we felt that Brahim had almost come to the end of the long round of bargaining that had begun the previous evening at the village of Ofira, a cluster of huts near Sharm el Sheikh and about nine miles east, where we had first made contact with him. Typical of most Arabs, the fisherman had named an exorbitant figure when he agreed to charter his felucca to us, after which we spent the entire evening drinking very sweet and strong black coffee out of tiny cups while slowly bringing down his price. Our haggling was a social game, often interrupted by talk of other things and filled with polite expressions and good wishes.

Now we were within a few shillings of the correct price, and although we would have willingly paid a little extra in order to conclude the transaction and get under way, we knew it would be impolite to do so and would, in addition, cause Brahim intense disappointment.

Nicholas Hawkins and I had been boyhood friends in Spain and had shared an abiding interest in the sea and in sharks, but we had lost contact in 1936, soon after the outbreak of the Spanish Civil War, neither knowing that the other was in Egypt until we met in hospital in Cairo after we had both been wounded. Coincidentally, each of us had elected to enlist as tank soldiers when World War II was declared, but whereas I was with the Royal Tank Regiment, Nick was with a Lancer unit. Recently, we had both engaged in the same battle against German armor, and we had become casualties within 24 hours of each other. My friend received a glancing wound on the right side of the head that had produced severe concussion, whereas I got a fragment of steel in the left calf that stubbornly refused to heal. We were granted four weeks of convalescent leave, and the doctor thought we might derive benefit from a sojourn by the sea. He had, of course, meant the Mediterranean, which was accessible to the north of Cairo, but we decided on the Red Sea so that we might once again take up our study of sharks while renewing our boyhood friendship. My twentieth birthday was two months away; Nicholas had celebrated his inside a tank in the Western Desert the previous February.

The day before our discharge from hospital, while waiting for the precious papers that would set us free for a month, we had planned our small expedition, pooling our money and making lists of the equipment we would require. First and foremost, we needed clothing, for we had lost every last bit of apparel when our respective tanks had caught fire and become gutted; this we could get easily and free of charge from the quartermaster, but then we needed fishing equipment, sufficient food to last until we returned to our regiments and various other items that the army would be extremely reluctant to furnish. The major one was transportation. We *had* to have a truck.

Even today, when new roads have been made and old ones improved, the Sinai is a tough country over which to motor. Bereft of trees, the desert, spiked here and there by camel thorn and scrub, marches naked along the flat and climbs the craggy mountains that begin just south of the port of El Shatt, opposite Egypt's Suez, then continue southward to congregate thickly before traveling north along the east coast. Wadis, stream beds that are mostly dry in summer and water-filled during the infrequent rains, crisscross the land. Many of these were unbridged in those days; a vehicle had to enter them, fight with the treacherous bottom and climb out again. Light vehicles bogged down quickly in such places, and even heavy desert trucks fitted with special tires needed sand tracks — lengths of flat, slotted steel that could be placed in front of the wheels to give traction and over which the truck climbed until it bogged down anew.

From Suez, where we proposed to enter the Sinai, to Ras Muhammad, we were going to have to negotiate about 200 miles of hard going during intense heat. A truck was a must; so were sand tracks and supplies of gasoline sufficient to take us there and bring us back; and enough drinking water to last between oases; and two rifles and ammunition for personal defense because small groups of isolated British Tommies were liable to be attacked by wandering bedouins for whom the war had brought only suffering and poverty and who, not unnaturally, did what their ancestors had been forced to do for centuries: help themselves whenever they got the chance.

None of the essential items could be procured officially, so it became necessary to scheme. Fortunately, my own unit, or what was left of it after our last action, was camped outside Cairo, waiting for new tanks and replacement crews; and when we left hospital and had obtained by legal means the kit to which we were entitled, we hitched our way to my tank squadron and sought aid from sympathetic listeners. By evening, we

had what we wanted, although there was some resistance from the sec-
ond-in-command, a dour army major who was at first opposed to our
scheme. Looking at us frowningly, he thought about our request, shook
his head, then said: "I say, boys, don't you think that divin' among sharks
is a rather dangerous business?"

The irony of his remark was completely lost on him until we both
burst out laughing, then he too guffawed.

"Yes, I take your point," he said afterward, "Gettin' shot out there
ain't too healthy either!"

Now, standing in the warm waters of the Red Sea and concluding
our bargaining with Brahim, the 200-mile trek across the wastes of Sinai
that took three days of hard, constant going was almost removed from
our minds. We were tired, of course, and not as fit as we might have
been, but despite the fact that Nick would occasionally get dizzy and my
wound continued to ooze bloody lymph, we were eager to commence
our small adventure and to forget the place and the times that we had
come from.

Our plan was to spend a week on the felucca, mostly fishing for
sharks so as to identify as many local species as we could, dissect them
and check the contents of their stomachs. After that, we were going to
camp at Sharm el Sheikh, where a wonderful reef exists that teems with
fascinating, multicolored fish, including a nocturnal species that blinks
light. Here we would spend ten days, then climb aboard the truck and
return to our units.

BRAHIM ABDULLAH's method for catching sharks was simple and direct,
as he demonstrated during the morning of our first day on board his
felucca. At the stern of the boat, bolted to a platform that was secured to
the deck, was a large drumlike reel operated by a crank that could be put
into free-dive to release line, but was controlled by a backlash-preventing
ratchet when a large fish was hooked. For bait, the Arab used any of the
abundant fish that could be taken almost for the asking; and he would
employ only newly caught specimens.

In this way, we hooked four black-tipped reef sharks in quick succession while trawling slowly off Tiran Island, in the strait of the same name. These selachians, abundant in many waters, were about four feet long and allowed themselves to be brought in quite readily. Gaffed and hauled up on deck, however, they lashed about furiously, snapping at anything that came within reach of their jaws until Brahim's crewman, a teenaged nephew, killed them by clubbing them on the head.

When the last black-tip had been boated, and because neither Nick nor I wished to spend an entire day cutting up sharks (we could not keep them overnight because the heat would quickly rot their internal organs), we decided to stop fishing until the catch had been disposed of. This immediately brought protests from the Arab, who told us that the population of sharks had increased greatly since the war, a circumstance brought about by the many ships sunk by U-boats in the Arabian Sea and Indian Ocean, each disaster taking its toll of human life. Attracted by the explosions and soon learning that these were followed by many blood trails that led to the dead and injured, sharks congregated in the general area. All it took to bring a dozen or more large specimens, said the Arab, was one small explosion. He added that he hated selachians because one had killed his brother, the father of our young crewman. Brahim explained that his brother had gone over the side to clear a fouled propeller one evening about a year earlier. Having done the job, the man rose to the surface and was about to climb on board again when he was struck and pulled under. The body was never recovered.

"Big, big shark," explained Brahim in his stilted English. "Much blood and more shark come soon. Nothing left of brother."

Recalling that conversation of so many years ago, I realize now that neither one of us showed much sympathy. And I regret that, for Brahim and his nephew were greatly moved by the account and were still grieving; but Nick and I, like all those who were involved in the desert war, had become inured to death to the extent that even the prospect of our own demise had ceased to have much of an effect on our emotions. Brahim noticed our rather callous attitude and he sulked at the tiller, steering us on course for Ras Abu Soma, on the Egyptian coast, where he said large sharks were to be found about a mile offshore. Meanwhile,

Nick and I dissected the black-tips, the last of which produced a discovery that put an end to the Arab's gloom.

The first shark, a male, had stuffed himself full of caranxes, which are large, silvery fish related to the jacks, pompanos, scads and horse mackerels. The second shark, a female, had eaten a sparse meal of assorted fish. The third, also female, was almost empty except for an unrecognizable lump of animal protein in which some fish bones and scales were discernible in addition to a piece of wooden dowel an inch thick by three inches long. The fourth shark, the second male, contained a surprise.

Nick was just washing his hands after dissecting his fish when I slit open the black-tip's stomach and reached into grasp a jellied object that was not recognizable as a human foot until I had removed it from its place in the gut. Dropping it hurriedly, I left it on the deck as I went to Nick's bucket of seawater to wash the residues from my right hand, explaining the nature of my discovery as I did so. Brahim, handing the tiller to his nephew, ran to look, bent down and stared intently, muttering a slurred "Bismillah!" Nick also came to see, then left for the rail, over which he hung until he finished retching.

This grizzly discovery somewhat marred our equanimity. The foot had belonged to an adult, probably a male, but it had been in the water for some time, having become jellied by the action of the salt. In places, the flesh had fallen away to reveal yellow bones; but where it remained, it was so soft that it cracked when it was disturbed.

The foot posed something of a problem, for its discovery ought to have been reported. On the other hand, we were in an area where no competent authority existed, and the heat and our lack of refrigeration precluded keeping the ghastly object. Brahim wanted nothing to do with the find. He was all for having it thrown overboard; and although Nick and I had by this time become more or less accustomed to the sight of dismembered humans, we shared our captain's distaste. After some discussion, we sewed the thing up in a piece of old canvas, weighted with bits and pieces of iron that Brahim carried for ballast, and we consigned it to the sea after reciting a portion of the burial service.

Chastened, we dumped the bodies of the sharks over the side without ceremony, and we then repaired to the dark, stifling and dingy cabin amidships and opened a bottle of whiskey. Brahim, though a Moslem, joined us, while his nephew continued to sail the felucca southward.

We had no means of knowing where the shark had picked up the foot, of course, but we felt certain that the body to which it belonged had not been killed by selachians, otherwise the flesh would have presented a very different appearance. We conjectured that the man had drowned, but where and how will never be known.

While the afternoon wore into evening, we remained below, drinking moderately and discussing our find while wondering if we should continue to fish for sharks from the boat. But, having already paid for the full week, and being intrigued by Brahim's insistence that large sharks would be encountered by morning, we conquered the scruples occasioned by our recent find. Later, on deck, under a clear star-studded sky in which a half-moon was visible, we watched the phosphorescent wake and listened to the many tales spun in broken English by the felucca's captain, all of which concerned sharks in one way or another.

At dawn the next day, as we breakfasted on sardines, hard-tack biscuits and tea while the felucca lay at anchor in the lee of Ras (cape) Abu Soma, Nick grinned hugely and suggested that we test Brahim's theory. When I asked him to what particular theory he was alluding, he gulped another mouthful of tea, sat pensive for some moments and nodded toward the cabin, where our equipment was stacked.

"The thing about an explosion bringing the big fish," he said. "We have grenades, don't we?"

For extra protection we had scrounged six hand grenades from my squadron armorer, each primed and fitted with a six-second fuse. As I was about to agree to the notion, our Arab skipper, hearing Nick's words, came over, grinning. He was delighted by the idea.

"Aiwah! Yes!" he said in both languages so as to leave no doubt that we would understand. "Make big booms, then shark come soon quick!"

After a brief conference, we decided we could spare two of the pineapple-type little bombs, but we also decided that if the first one had the forecasted and desired effect, we would not pull the pin on the sec-

ond, for we *were* expected to account for the things on our return and
there was always the chance that we might have to use them for our own
protection during our journey back.

Waiting impatiently for the sun to climb into the sky, we sat at the
stern. Nick, who had a stopwatch, was ready to time the interval
between the explosion and the arrival of the sharks, if they came at all. I
would pull the pin and throw the bomb without any count, so that it
would sink a respectable distance below the surface before going off, thus
muffling the explosion above the water and being less likely to damage
some part of the rather ancient craft that would furnish our only protection in the event the Arab was proven right in his surmise.

By full sun-up we had sailed into deep water about one and a half
miles from shore and from the village of Bur Safaga, for we didn't want
to alarm the inhabitants. Brahim and his nephew furled the sails; the
boat was allowed to drift on the calm sea. Now we were ready.

Standing at the stern, Nick zeroed the stopwatch and I prepared to
pull the pin from the grenade. Brahim had already baited a large fish
caught that morning on an enormous hook connected to a heavy line by
a six-foot length of chain. I pulled the pin, used a cricket lob to throw
the bomb, watched as it arched through space and then entered the
water with an audible plop about 60 yards astern. It was not a good
throw. I began to count slowly. When I reached five, the dull boom of
the explosion filled the Arabs with joy almost at the moment that a small
eruption broke the calm surface. Nick activated his watch.

Every pair of eyes on board scanned the surface of the sea in all
directions as the circular waves created by the explosion reached the boat,
rocking her slightly as they passed under us. Three minutes and twenty-
eight seconds after the explosion, about 20 dead fish floated upward,
most of them small and a brilliant orange-red. We were unable to identify them; they looked like a species called *Anthiases*, but I don't believe
these fish stray far from reefs. But inasmuch as we didn't manage to
recover any of them, I am unable to be sure of their identity.

We had intended to climb into the dinghy, which was tied astern,
and to pick up some specimens, but as we were about to go over the side,

Brahim uttered a loud cry and pointed south, almost dancing with excitement. Looking in the direction his finger pointed, we saw a small armada of dorsal fins, most of them of medium size but two that were large. Nick, always a cool-head, looked at his watch: the sharks had arrived within seven minutes and nine seconds of the explosion; that is to say, they had come to the surface within that time, but whether they had already been keeping station in the area or had come from farther afield, we could not determine.

Brahim was delighted, of course. Not only had his forecast been proven but now he was being permitted to cast his baited hook over the side, though not before he had started the incredibly old donkey engine that pushed the felucca along at about four knots when needed. The wheezy gasoline motor, sitting in a well in the afterdeck and almost float-ing in a mixture of oil, gas and seawater, sputtered and stuttered as the fisherman turned the crank handle; it fired, died, fired again and at last began to propel the felucca toward the scissoring dorsals.

During all this, I had been counting fins, reaching 23 by the time Brahim cast the chain over the side at the same moment that his nephew released the line. On we went, our attention centered on one of the big sharks, our tensions rising as a number of the lesser fry changed direction and came toward us. Nick, wanting desperately to hook into a big fish, dashed away and returned with one of our Lee-Enfield rifles, working the bolt so as to put a shell in the breech and standing guard at the stern, intending to shoot at any small shark that went for the bait. This was a useless gesture, as he himself realized moments later, for the bait was already too deep to be seen, and any one of the smaller sharks on the sur-face, or others that had not yet come up, could easily grab the hook without our knowledge, out of range of the rifle.

Nick was about to unload but Brahim urged him to shoot, making us understand in a mixture of Arabic and English that the death strug-gles of one of their number would cause the sharks to go into a frenzy.

It had been said that sharks avoid the flesh of their own kind, that they are in some way repelled by it. Having confirmed this for myself a number of times, I know that this opinion is valid, but, like so many generalizations applied to selachians, it has been exaggerated. That is to say, the use of shark meat as bait is only likely to attract scavenger sharks, such as dogfish and others that are predominantly bottom feeders, but a live shark that has been wounded and is going through the death struggles is almost sure to be attacked by other sharks. Being ignorant of these things at the time, and since Brahim had so far proved himself knowledgeable, Nick sighted the Enfield on a small dorsal and squeezed the trigger.

Immediately following the explosion, the target shark convulsed and began to thrash wildly, blood coming from a body wound and spreading quickly on the surface. Before the report had stopped ringing in our ears, bedlam erupted in the water. I was watching intently through binoculars. The distance was less than 100 yards, and I had a good focus on the injured shark, which was turning in circles at one instant and showing its belly, and at the next its back, dorsal and tail fins. Suddenly a medium-sized selachian came up from below, its jaws wide; it fastened itself to the injured shark's body at a point between the caudal and the dorsal, closing the gape and shaking violently. I had time to see blood flow from each jagged puncture before another, somewhat smaller shark struck, disembowelling its relative and swimming away gulping intestines and parts of the stomach wall. One after another, the sharks struck, bloodying the water and making the surface look as though it was boiling. According to Nick's stopwatch, the six-foot shark was torn to pieces in one minute and eleven seconds. All that remained of it was the blood, and even this was soon dissipated.

Now Brahim turned the felucca and steered so as to pass through the frenzied mob, but the big dorsals had disappeared. It was starting to look as though we would have to settle for a smaller shark.

Nick was sitting on the stern rail, holding the rifle in his left hand, when a shark struck the baited hook with such force that the boat shuddered. If I hadn't put out a steadying hand, my friend would have gone overboard. Brahim and his nephew were yelling themselves hoarse, screaming Arabic words that were unintelligible while line began to peel off the drum at such speed that it caused the whole mechanism to squeal. Fortunately, the handle was freewheeling, for the nephew had not engaged it after his uncle tossed the bait overboard and allowed the line to peel off; otherwise, I feel sure the whole thing would have been wrenched out of the boat.

As I was wondering how we were going to stop the wildly spinning drum, Brahim approached carrying a much-chewed wooden pole. He thrust it between the outside of the metal drum and the heavy, iron stanchion that housed and supported the axle. The pole, while not stopping the revolutions, acted as a brake. This was clearly the method employed by the Arab when faced with such a situation. Gradually, smoke coming from the wood, the drum began to lose speed. Soon, it was barely turning. The nephew picked up a short iron bar and used it to release the spring-loaded ratchet, yelling loudly as he did so. This was evidently a signal, for Brahim dropped the pole and grabbed the handle, easing the strain on the ratchet and immediately thereafter starting to turn it, winding so as to retrieve line against the struggling fish.

The iron handle of the winch was two feet long, so I hurried to Brahim's assistance. Now the line became bar-taut and shed a fine spray of water as it very slowly came in. Nick worked the rifle bolt, ready to deliver the coup de grâce if the monster secured to the hook could be hauled in without snapping the line, something we both suspected it would do.

By this time, Nick was so excited he forgot to time the action; but we both estimated that after about 15 minutes, the shark showed signs of tiring. The handle became so easy to turn that Brahim left me to it while he went to the motor and opened the throttle as wide as it would go, an action that caused no noticeable increase in our speed but which I presume was undertaken so as to counteract the pull of the captive. Presently the Arab told me to stop turning the handle, to allow the boat to pull the struggling shark.

"He get bloody tired this way. Very much bloody tired," our skipper proclaimed.

By now, if Brahim Abdullah had announced that the shark would swim on board of its own accord, I think we would have believed him, but on this occasion the Arab's forecast was incorrect. The felucca, its engine working at full stroke, pumping greasy smoke that bubbled out of the sea at our stern, accelerated our progress not one whit. And the shark continued to pull, seesawing the line first to port, then to starboard, jerking so violently that the stern shuddered with each pull.

In this way, we must have spent another ten minutes, but then, without warning, the line went slack. Too late did Brahim and his nephew try to get the canvas spread to give us more speed, for the shark was now swimming in the same direction as we were heading. As the two worked at the ropes, Nick and I dived for the handle and started to wind in line as fast as we were able, meeting no resistance until as suddenly as the big fish had spurted forward, it swung to starboard, racing away but rising so that its big, triangular dorsal broke the surface. From a distance of about 100 yards, we heard the hiss as the fin cleaved through the water, but then we became too busy to listen or watch as the stern shuddered anew and the shark began to pull as hard as ever. Yet we were gaining; yard by yard the line was wound around the drum and now we could see the dorsal and caudal fins clearly enough to identify the monster as a white-tipped shark (*Carcharhinus longimanus*), its general coloring gray-brown and the distinctive white, almost round spots on the dorsal and pectoral fins unmistakable.

Nick, who could be rather exuberant, announced that he was sure the shark was "at least 16 feet long!" Although the creature was large, my estimate was about 14 feet. The white-tip was now clearly tiring, but every now and then, it would turn to face the boat and make a short run, whereupon Nick and I wound in as much free line as we had time for. Staying at starboard, the big fish tried to regain lost sea room but it didn't attempt to dive. And then it stopped fighting. It came in, gaping, the big hook firmly caught on the left side of its mouth, its point protruding at the corner of the jaw; the teeth were erect and gleaming wickedly. Moments later, the animal was only about 20 yards away.

Brahim and the boy hauled down the sails; the engine was put into neutral. Leaving Nick at the handle, I picked up the Lee-Enfield, wrapped the sling around my right arm for support and aimed as best I could while standing on the heaving deck, my target the top of the great, broad head, where I knew the brain reposed just under the cartilage. I missed the brain but shot the shark through the eye, the impact of the .303 bullet stunning the animal. I quickly ejected the spent shell, put in a fresh one and tried again. This time I was right on the mark. The big body shivered, the round head raised itself out of the water, and then the massive animal went limp, blood oozing out of its two wounds and leaving a carmine trail that immediately attracted about a dozen lesser sharks, several of which appeared to be about eight feet long. None of these, however, dared approach the stricken monarch, and they turned away when the white-tip reached the side of our boat.

An hour later, the shark, a male, had been hauled on board and lay dead, stretched out on deck. Nevertheless, we kept clear of it for some time longer, just to be absolutely certain it was lifeless.

Looking at the body, I realized that the dorsal fin, though essentially triangular, had a rounded tip and was set slightly ahead of the center; the white spot was about six inches in diameter, more or less circular and contrasting with the gray of the rest of the fin. The fish was 12 feet 10 inches long from the end of its caudal to the tip of its rather blunt, heavy snout. The body was more rounded than those of most selachians and of wide girth, but because it was now flat on the deck, I could only estimate the natural diameter at its widest point at about three feet. The eyes were small, somewhat piglike, the undamaged orb having an extremely sinister appearance even in death. The white-spotted pectoral fins were very long, blunt at the ends and wide where they joined the body.

On the whole, this shark presented a powerful appearance, and we were not surprised it had put up such a monstrous fight. It was the largest shark I had seen until then, and when I later examined its enormous mouth and the vicious inch-and-a-half-long teeth, I was greatly impressed. Today, I would have regretted killing such an animal, but at the time, I was too preoccupied with its size and anatomy, not to mention with my apprehension of it, to give its death much thought. Undoubtedly, it was a magnificent being. I don't believe now that we had the right to end its life.

Amazingly, when we opened his stomach, it was empty. There was not even a trace of a meal! But the liver was enormous and must have weighed 100 pounds. Brahim salvaged this to sell or reclaim the oil, stuffing it into a steel drum over which he secured a lid and, helped by his nephew, he took it down into the hold. Since that liver had to remain on board for several days before the Arab disposed of it, I hated to think what the smell would have been like at the time! Knowing nothing about the processing of oil from shark livers, the stench may be routine; if so, I am happy in my ignorance!

The next day, urged by Nick, Brahim and his nephew, I tossed one more grenade into the sea, but on this occasion, only small- to medium-sized sharks came to investigate. There was one white-tip, but this one only measured about eight feet in length. Nevertheless, we caught six more selachians, investigated them, checked their stomach contents and allowed Brahim to add their livers to the already smelly barrel.

That evening, the weather turned nasty and we returned to Ras Muhammad to find shelter in the bay, thankful we could stretch our legs ashore. Strolling over the sand, Nick and I decided we had had enough of shark fishing and especially of the odorous felucca. We asked Brahim to run us to Ofira in the morning, and there, collecting our truck from its guardian — another of our fisherman's relations — we found a camping place at Sharm el Sheikh and began to dive on the reef.

OUR CHILDHOOD experiences with sharks had prepared us for dealing with the fish that we had caught in the Red Sea, but with the memory of the large white-tip fresh in our minds, we felt some apprehension as we were about to make our first dive in the area of the reef. I suppose we should have realized that we would encounter large sharks in these waters. Now as we faced the dive, we remembered the precautions we had taken years earlier in Spain when, after I had been scraped by one of our captive specimens, I had cut myself a stick, shod its end with an upside-down soft-drink cap and used it to prod away any sharks that seemed to want to make body contact.

At Sharm el Sheikh we had no soft drinks, but we did have some bottled beer, so we each cut a stout, two-inch-thick stick about three feet long and nailed an inverted beer cap on the bottom. The serrated edge of the crimped metal was rough enough to engage with the denticles of a shark and thus keep it at bay and arm's length.

Diving and keeping back to back, we found that for the 90 seconds we could hold our breath under water, we were able to concentrate on the exotic inhabitants of the reef. I shall always regret that we did not have enough knowledge to identify all the species we encountered; but when we first saw an enormous school of *Anthiases* and swam amongst them, we had no difficulty recognizing them from illustrations we had seen in books. What a sight they were! Hundreds upon hundreds of small corally-orange fish, perhaps as long as a large goldfish but more oval and basslike, darted along en masse, opening their ranks to swim around us but otherwise not at all nervous. If we clung to the coral and remained still, some of the inquisitive little fish would dart up to us and examine our faces while others would nibble gently at our toes, but as soon as we moved, they dashed away and stampeded the entire shoal. Yet they never went far, wheeling like well-drilled calvary and then continuing to meander over, under and around the coral.

So engrossed did we become with the *Anthiases* that we forgot about sharks for two days; but when we dived into another area of the reef, where the water was deep and purple blue, we found ourselves almost surrounded by small black-tips, at least five or six dozen of them. Seven or eight of these immediately came to investigate us, and two, bolder than the others, came in for a bite, their mouths open and their rubbery snouts elevated. They were only about four feet long, but we already knew that even a very small shark could be dangerous, so we backed into the coral and fended them off with our sticks until it was time to rise for air.

Now, unable to watch our feet and having to go up quickly, we felt vulnerable, but we reached the surface without mishap. There, treading water and trying to see if anything was aiming at our white and temptingly flashing feet, we thought it might be better to go ashore and consider new strategy; but as we turned to swim back, a distance of about

100 yards, a number of the reef sharks rose to the surface while others gathered below our legs. To stay where we were was unquestionably dangerous; to swim back appeared equally perilous. There was no choice, however, so we kept together and struck out, moving in a measured way and forcing ourselves to look at the land rather than try to see into the water. Twice we were brushed lightly by sharks, but no blood was spilled, except for what must have been a minute amount of my own juices that leaked from under the dressing.

On shore, unhurt and relieved, we discussed our recent predicament and decided that if we could rent a rowboat in Ofira, we could go out in it to dive, anchoring it and having it available as a refuge if we should again be faced by a host of selachians or by one of the large *longimanus*.

That evening, we managed to rent an old wooden, lapstrake dinghy with two oars and enough rope for the anchor to reach bottom just off the edge of the reef. For the remainder of our stay, we used it as planned.

One afternoon toward the end of our second week in the Sinai, I dived alone, for Nick had been getting dizzy spells and we felt that the constant change of pressure was probably responsible for his attacks. He remained in the boat; but because the water was so beautifully clear, he could watch me, so we thought it would be safe for me to go down unaccompanied.

In these days of sophisticated diving equipment, few may know that free diving consists of innumerable up-and-down journeys and many frustrations, for it seemed that when I was most interested in something, my lungs could no longer be denied oxygen. It was thus on that afternoon, for no sooner had I gone down when I saw two reef sharks, a male and a female, engaged in rather strange behavior. The male was about six feet long; he kept rubbing into the female, who was a foot longer. She was quite placid, but the male was obviously agitated. I had just concluded that I was about to witness the mating behavior of sharks when I had to rise. Pausing only long enough to tell Nick what I had seen, I went down again and this time saw the two, some distance away now, swimming side by side in circles, the male acting most aggressively. Holding onto a knob of coral, I watched through the goggles, cursing the distance and the dancing light that made it hard to see; but even as I was doing so, the two sharks came closer.

The female circled away from the male, as though seeking to avoid him, whereupon he turned and attacked her, biting her on the body at a place just ahead of the dorsal fin and inflicting what appeared to be a serious wound; yet she didn't seem to mind or feel pain. Indeed, she swam closer to her mate, and he bit her again, higher up the body, near the head. Twice more he struck her, the last bite being inflicted on the left pectoral fin, tearing it. Now I had to rise. Anxious to get air and to come down again, I kicked away from the coral and allowed myself to go up more quickly than usual.

As I was nearing the bottom of the dinghy, an oar was struck violently on the water, its blade flat, the report and concussion only about four or five feet over my head. Clearly Nick was doing this, but I could not imagine why. Before I had time to inquire, the oar struck again and yet again. Now, warned by some instinct, I looked down.

The larger of the two sharks was coming straight for me. She was only about 20 feet away. As she advanced, I moved more quickly than I had ever done, reaching up even before my head was out of the water and feeling Nick's hands close over my own. He heaved and I scrambled, and I rolled into the boat as the shark rammed against the bottom.

Twice did the enraged shark hit our fragile boat, then we upped anchor and got away from there. On shore, we noticed that the rough shark skin had scraped the bottom in places until it showed new wood, and one of the laps had cracked.

Nick told me later that he had seen me start up just as the female shark turned to follow. Fortunately, it had stayed below at first, circling cautiously, but as I was nearing the boat, it had accelerated, aiming for my legs. That was when Nick had taken the oar and used it to slap the water, hoping to scare it away. It didn't have any effect on the shark, but it surely had an effect on me! For that I shall always be grateful to Nicholas Hawkins.

The next day we both went down, but on our second dive, we raced toward the boat when a long, sinister shape slowly materialized from the deep water. Soon we could identify the shark: it was a blue, perhaps even longer than the white-tip we had caught. Blue sharks are dangerous, so we lost little time in quitting the sea. Even so, the incredibly beautiful fish, its back and flanks almost as aquamarine as the water, circled our dinghy several times, no more than 15 feet away. This gave us a ringside seat, and because the animal was so calm and had its teeth folded back, I felt it was merely curious.

Would this great fish really attack? Nick said yes; I felt it would not. To settle the argument, I went over the side but held onto the boat. The blue continued to circle, a placid master of the sea, in no way agitated. Nick handed me the shark stick. I took it but didn't think such a puny weapon would be of much use against the long fish. Nevertheless, since we were near the reef and there were many nooks and crannies to duck into in an emergency, I decided to dive, stilling Nick's protests by asking him to row the boat nearer to the shallow part of the reef so I could climb into it faster if the need arose.

That was one of the most memorable dives of my life. The blue stopped circling the moment I went under but he didn't approach at first. Standing off and patrolling a course parallel to the coral, he turned, lazy and fluid and gorgeous, and came back, edging closer yet keeping about ten feet between us.

Now I was in 20 feet of water, and Nick had brought the dinghy to a point almost above my head, so I felt more secure and certain that the blue shark had no intention of attacking. I swam away from the coral toward the long fish; he moved back, not afraid but not willing to be approached beyond the boundaries he had set. For about half a minute, we swam side by side, then I had to turn and go back, rising beside the boat. The shark came closer, reached the shallow water and turned away anew.

Four times I went down and the blue continued to exhibit curiosity, but never once did he show himself disposed to attack. And every time I edged closer to him, he turned away, his movements so coordinated that I would never get tired of watching them. Indeed, while I was down with him, it occurred to me that to have a huge aquarium, one side made of glass and built into the wall of a room, would produce an observation chamber where a person could be calmed by simply watching the lovely motions of a great blue shark!

That night, although the moon was made gibbous by the wane, the skies were so clear and the light so brilliant that we decided to dive in one of the shallower areas of the reef so as to watch the luminous display of a strange little fish called *Photoblepharon* that has a light cell beneath each eye and folds of skin that can be raised or lowered over each luminous organ. We had already seen their ghostly and most beautiful display from above the surface, but we felt that our visit would not be complete without going into the water.

Diving in shark waters at night without lights is risky, for man is blind and senseless while sharks can see near the surface if there is a moon, and they also have other devices to detect prey. But we thought that if we didn't go far from the shallower parts of the reef and had the boat handy as a refuge, we would at least be relatively safe.

By midnight, when the moon hung overhead, we went down, anxious to see the authors of the flashing lights that we had been admiring from the shore, winking, blue-green emanations that came and went constantly, sometimes in isolated, single flashes, more often in clustered bursts, so many that they could not be counted.

Below the water, hanging onto the coral, we were fascinated with the display and thrilled when several of the fish came near enough for us to see the outline of their bodies. These stayed near us so long as we didn't move; but as soon as the need for air drove us upward, every little eye-light in our neighborhood blinked out, covered by the folds of skin. Yet as we rose, we could still see hundreds of other flashes, some clear and bright, others mere glows that occurred everywhere along the reef. It was a magic lantern show, and although I have only witnessed it that one time from under the surface, it is still clear in my mind.

We observed that the *Photoblepharons* had luminous lateral lines, gill and eye edges, though these were not noticeable until the fish rose closer to the moonlight. The undersides, especially along the upper parts of the belly, also appeared to have luminous properties. For three hours, we dived to observe this enchanting and captivating fish.

My experiences in the Red Sea were to become invaluable in later years. At that time, I did not understand their significance and considered the adventure a pleasant way to spend a leave and to forget the war.

THE MAKO SHARK IS WIDESPREAD IN THE
ATLANTIC, PACIFIC AND OFF THE AUSTRALIAN COAST.
IT ACHIEVES A LENGTH OF UP TO 12 FEET AND
A WEIGHT IN EXCESS OF 1,000 POUNDS.

# Chapter 3

❦

DURING A second visit to Sharm el Sheikh in early 1942, I spent ten days observing the reef and its colorful inhabitants, including, once again, many black-tipped sharks. As before, all of these predators were about four feet long and just as active as they had been during my visit with Nick, who was killed in action on November 24, 1941, two months after our Sinai journey.

I restricted my activities to the shallower parts of the reef, staying close to the jagged coral and keeping a sharp eye on any black-tips that appeared interested in my movements. These sharks are found throughout the world's temperate and tropical seas, favoring reefs and shallows during most of the year, but retreating into somewhat deeper areas in winter in those regions where inshore waters cool during that season. In the Red Sea, however, because the temperature is always high, the black-tips are year-round residents of the reef. Members of this species are fast and agile and differ from most other sharks in that they are given to biting at prey during the first pass and without warning. This contrasts with the majority of their relatives, which usually make at least one exploratory pass and telegraph their intentions by wagging their heads from side to side. Thus I treated the black-tips with great respect. Although these fish rarely grow longer than eight feet, they are voracious feeders that travel in packs and, as I had already experienced in these waters, are likely to attack without provocation. Nevertheless, because I had come here (with great difficulty) to study sharks, I was determined to do just that! But I had decided even before arriving that I would immediately rent a rowboat from which to work, and I would never go down without a shark club.

Unlike my journey with Nick, when we had our own transportation, on this occasion I had hitched a ride with a military convoy that was taking supplies to Elat, at the landward end of the Gulf of Aqaba, in Palestine. Our route was through the middle of the Sinai Peninsula, a rugged track that threaded its way between mountain passes for some 150 miles. This journey lasted three days.

When I reached Elat, I bribed my way on a Jordanian fishing boat that was sailing south on the evening tide, stopping at Nuweiba, Dahab and Ofira, near Sharm el Sheikh, before going to fish the Red Sea. And since I had nothing better to do while the dhow chugged along at about eight knots, I occupied myself during the 140-mile sea journey by trolling for sharks, much to the surprise of the captain of the boat and three-man crew, who could not understand why a British soldier should want to catch such worthless fish, albeit the bearded skipper was quite willing to take the shark livers off my hands.

Before leaving, I had procured about a dozen good-sized caranxes to use as bait, storing them in the unrefrigerated hold; but since I caught nothing the first day out, the strike I got early the next morning was made on a far-from-fresh fish, perhaps accounting for the fact that I caught a tiger shark, for these selachians do not appear to dislike anything that is in the least edible. Having hooked the seven-foot fish, however, I found myself in somewhat the same predicament as the proverbial dog that chased a steamroller and, having caught it, did not know what to do with it!

As its kind go, that tiger wasn't a big one; but because I had no winch or even a heavy-duty fishing reel, I had to fight the shark by pulling on the manila rope to which was attached the chain leader that held the hook; and because I wasn't really expecting a strike, I was unprepared for it when it came. As a result, the rope was pulled through my hands so rapidly that it left burn marks on both palms.

If I had not previously secured the free end to a stanchion, the captive would have escaped, taking all my gear with it to wherever it is that tigers go when they're trying to rid themselves of a hook and a couple hundred feet of line! Even so, the shark stretched the manila so tightly that I felt sure it was going to break, which it probably would have done but for the fact that the fish, finding itself brought up short, leaped out of the water. This allowed me enough time to recover some slack that I doubled and snubbed around the afterdeck rail. Despite this, I believe the furious shark would have broken free had it not been for two crew members who came to help. After struggling for about 20 minutes, we got the tiger to the side and tied the rope fast. At this point, the crewmen allowed me the honor of killing it with a lily iron, no mean feat considering that the dhow had not slackened speed and that the distance from the deck to the water varied between four and eight feet in response to the pitching of the vessel.

Tying a rope around my waist and securing this to the rail, I leaned downward as far as I could and waited for a chance to harpoon the still furious tiger. Three times I struck and missed, but on the fourth try, the iron entered the shark's head, killing it almost instantly.

After my volunteer helpers joined me in pulling up the catch, I regretted my action. Looking at its sleek, elegant form and noting the sheen of its mottled skin as it captured the sunlight and cast it back in hundreds of starlike reflections, I found myself admiring the shark and marveling at its enormous strength. For the very first time in my adult life, I questioned my right to kill an animal so wantonly, feeling that by doing so, I had made ugly a being that in its own world reflected the beauty and creativity of nature. Occupied by these thoughts, I stood by the rail, legs spread to counterbalance the roll and pitch of the dhow while at the same time absorbing my surroundings. The Gulf of Aqaba is about 12 miles wide for the first two-thirds of its inland course, and as we were sailing through the middle of the channel, the coasts of Jordan and Sinai were clearly visible, the shorelines bereft of human habitation where only gulls were risking the lethal heat of the morning.

The sea and the panorama of desert and mountain, the blazing

African sun and the dead selachian combined to deepen my feelings of guilt, but I couldn't understand why I should so suddenly become upset because I had killed a shark. This caused me to become angry at myself, and I sought to rationalize my action on the grounds that selachians are dangerous animals and, as I believed at the time, devoid of feelings. But try as I might, I could not contemplate the dead tiger shark without experiencing regret.

Turning about, I leaned on the stern rail and stared at the Sinai mountains. Confusion gave way to unaccustomed gloom as my thoughts turned to Nick — more particularly to his death. I had collected his personal papers from the hospital and sent them to his family together with a letter expressing condolences, but I had felt no emotion while doing so. Now, smelling the acrid, ammoniac odor being given off by the dead shark and looking at the green sea and the cerulean sky, I realized that during my years of war, I had never been emotionally affected by the death of any man, friend *or* foe.

I was then almost 21 years old. I had first become exposed to war in Spain, when I was not yet 15. At no time had I felt either guilt or regret when faced with somebody's death, perhaps because I had quickly learned by observing others that a soldier who mourned another man's demise made himself vulnerable to a similar fate, the ensuing emotions tending to cloud his judgment and slow his reflexes.

Evidently, without conscious awareness, I became inured to the death of my fellows; and although I was outwardly gregarious and companionable, I was always careful to guard against the ties of friendship. For the enemy I felt neither hate nor sympathy. Only five weeks before I had caught the tiger shark that had precipitated my present brooding, I had directed fire on an enemy tank and had seen its commander emerge from within the turret, his body enveloped in flames. He had fallen on the sand, bleeding and burning and thrashing about violently in the agony of dying while his crew became incinerated within the vehicle. Rolling past the blazing tank, I noted that two of our armor-piercing projectiles had scored hits, one entering through the front of the hull, the other through the turret. Even above the rattle and squeak of our caterpillar treads, I could hear the ammunition exploding, feeding the fire. Yet I felt only satisfaction at the elimination of an enemy tank and five of its crew. Two days later, my own tank was hit by gunfire. Three of my crew were killed instantly. My turret gunner escaped unhurt. I was hit in the neck by a piece of metal. Again, no emotion. I had once more emerged relatively unscathed. I thought fondly of a time in hospital between clean sheets, of food that had no sand mixed in it, of relief from the heat by day and the cold by night, for the desert temperature drops dramatically after sundown. But, most of all, I thought of leave, of coming here to do what I had just done, to catch and kill sharks, to dissect them and to study them.

These memories allowed me to return to what I then considered to be my normal state of mind. My guilt evaporated as I began to open the tiger, a male that had eaten a number of unrecognizable fish in addition to some assorted, inedible flotsam, including the brass casing from a 20-millimeter cannon shell, no doubt picked up at sea while a naval vessel had been firing at an attacking aircraft.

Afterward, having removed the shark's liver and opened its head so as to examine its brain and, particularly, the wound inflicted on it by the lily iron, I threw the remains over the side after cutting off some pieces of meat to use as bait, for I was then under the impression that the majority of sharks were greedy for the flesh of their own kind. Tossing the rotting caranxes overboard, I continued to troll, but I failed to get another strike.

The next day I was put off at Ofira, where I managed to rent a rowboat. Except that it was similar in construction and design, the four-meter craft was a vast improvement on the one Nick and I had rented, being newer and having both storage lockers and three excellent oars. I loaded my equipment into the forward section and rowed the short distance to Sharm el Sheikh, making camp on the sands and finding that the stick shelter Nick and I had constructed on our first visit was still in place, a shield against the scorching sun. Nearby, I was delighted to find one of the shark sticks we had made.

When my camp was in order, I dug a deep hole within the shade of the shelter, and into this I put the three five-gallon freshwater jerry cans that I had brought with me and had filled at Ofira, for there was no stream or well in the vicinity of Sharm el Sheikh. Placing the water below the grade kept it more or less cool during the sun hours and allowed it to cool further overnight, otherwise my drinking supply would have always remained at a warm-tepid temperature.

When these tasks were completed, I had supper and afterward cleaned the Thompson submachine gun that I had brought with me for defense against the possibility of confrontation with one of the marauding bands of bedouins that sometimes preyed on defenseless individuals. But such an attack was far more likely to occur en route, rather than in the Sharm el Sheikh area, which was sparsely occupied by Arabs who subsisted by fishing and growing vegetables. Indeed, the people Nick and I had met here, and whom I now encountered anew, were kindly and helpful, if rather puzzled by the *Inglisi* who wanted to study sharks.

Later, under a sky ablaze with stars, I sat on a rock at water's edge and watched the Red Sea, listening to its murmurs and splashes, enjoying the slightly acrid scent of its waters and once again admiring the quick bursts of blue-green light emitted by the little *Photoblepharon* fish, the scientific name for which was unknown to me then. (In fact, the Linnean or Latin names of almost all of the species that I encountered in that area were unknown to me, for I had not yet engaged in formal biological studies. In any event, many species of fish as well as sharks were still unknown to science, including the *Photoblepharon*, which were not studied and classified until recent years. For these reasons, the species that are named in this narrative have been determined by what may be termed hindsight. That is to say, by consulting notes made at the time, by memory and by researching the literature, I have managed to identify those fish for which the scientific names are included in italic type.)

Early on the morning after my arrival at the edge of the reef, I began diving in relatively shallow water, alternating between observing the marine life and, wherever possible, collecting small fish, worms, crabs and other small marine organisms and carrying them to the surface. There, reverting to my childhood practices, I made small pools into which I released the captives, thereafter studying them as best I could, noting physical and habitual characteristics before releasing them. My observations had to be concluded within an hour or so because the temperature was such that the little pools soon became too hot for their occupants, a fact I discovered when the first group died after I left them while I made additional dives.

In the course of that first day, I saw many black-tipped sharks, but because I remained close to the reef and was never deeper than about ten feet, all but one ignored me. The exception was only three feet long, but it attacked me on three separate occasions during my afternoon dives.

I had been trying to hand-net a small barracuda that was eluding me by sheltering among the coral interstices when I first became aware of the small shark's approach. Seeming to materialize out of nowhere, the black-tip darted in from above and made a swift pass at the hand net, which, white as it was, and billowing lazily in the water, had evidently attracted the predator. Before I could lift the club in order to fend off my visitor, it struck the handle of the net, its teeth grating on the wood some three inches in front of my knuckles. Grasping the wood, it shook its head twice, but as I resisted, the handle slipped out of its mouth, breaking off two or three teeth. Now the shark veered away, going upward but staying in my vicinity, swimming in circles. As it was doing so, I rolled up the net and stuck the light-colored material inside my swimming trunks so as to remove the temptation. Then I rose to the surface, keeping as near to the jagged reef as I could.

During my next dive, I went down without the net, but the shark was nowhere to be seen. The little barracuda, nevertheless, was still poking about in its earlier location, so I returned topside to get the net and dived again. This time I managed to catch the small fish, which was about eight inches long, but I was not given a chance to study it because, as I was turning away with the fish entangled in the folded net, the black-tip again swooped down, grabbed the net, shook its head and turned away, swallowing the material and its occupant. Again I rose, now rather annoyed with the shark, but nevertheless cautious. On the surface

I picked up the four-foot hand harpoon that I had brought along, and with this and the shark club, which dangled by a thong from my left wrist, I descended again, planning to search for another small barracuda but determined to put an end to the shark if it interfered anew. My annoyance stemmed from the fact that, although I had brought a small roll of spare netting with which to repair the scoop when it became torn, the black-tip had virtually eaten the entire baglike container. This meant that, instead of sewing a patch over a hole or cut, I had to fashion a complete net and attach it to its wire hoop, a laborious job when performed with the few tools I had.

Exploring the area of reef where I had caught the ill-fated specimen, I soon saw two more of its kind, both about the same size. Of the black-tip there was no sign. Pleased, I turned to rise, planning to immediately make a new net. Even as I moved, the small shark charged me, coming so quickly from the rear that I didn't realize it was there until its body scraped against my leg. I was lucky! It seemed that because I was close to the coral, the black-tip had been forced to turn away before it could fasten its jaws on my calf. As it was, the sandpaper hide scraped my flesh and resulted in an abrasion two inches long by about one inch wide that bled immediately.

Kicking off from the sand, I started rising just as the shark came at me again. As I raised the harpoon and aimed it at the approaching fish, I noticed three more of its kind hovering about 20 feet away, but I had no time to worry about them just then, for the charging shark literally impaled itself on the harpoon head. While these things were occurring, I had continued rising, and seconds later my head broke the surface. The impaled black-tip, meanwhile, was fighting the harpoon, while I hung onto the handle, for I was determined to get that fish ashore and make sure it would never bother me or anybody else again. Even so, before I could lift the shark from the water, another of its kind struck its side, scooping out a piece of belly and about a foot of intestines. But the shark was far from dead! I scrambled on shore.

Walking toward one of the larger pools that I had made, I stopped beside it long enough to pull the harpoon out of the black-tip's chest area, after which I put the fish into the pool. Bleeding, trailing parts of its mangled intestines, and holed by the harpoon at a point between the back of the mouth and the first gill slit, that black-tip shark remained alive in the pool for 37 hours, despite its fatal injuries and the excessive warmth of the water! Surprisingly, the shark appeared to be unaware of its wounds as it swam casually within the confines of the pool.

The next morning, several hours before it died, I noticed that some of the partially digested remains of the barracuda it had stolen from me were actually spilling out of its side into the water, emerging from a slit in its duodenum. No other animal I know of could have sustained such injuries for so long. Although the little shark had tried to bite me, I could not blame it for responding to its primal urges, and I could not help but respect its superb endurance and the confidence it had displayed in its own prowess when it dared to attack a creature twice its length and more than seven times its weight.

Remembering the young sharks I had kept as a child, I found myself hoping that the black-tip, a male, would somehow manage to survive his injuries, experiencing a somewhat nostalgic sense of déjà vu as I recalled the frequent occasions when I had squatted beside a rocky pool in Mallorca while I sought to get a moribund shark to take food.

Today, looking back on that experience at Sharm el Sheikh, I believe the small black-tip was responsible for rekindling the great fascination that *living* animals had for me during my formative years. Always I had become upset when one of my charges died, and although I was too young to realize that captivity had almost invariably been responsible for the demise of each, I did get a *sense* that prolonged imprisonment might have been at least partly responsible for the high mortality rate among my pets. From then on, I kept sharks and fish for short periods, observing them, playing with some of the more tractable specimens and then, regretfully, returning them to the sea.

When the black-tip died, I felt a sense of personal loss, probably because, being completely alone, I had unconsciously associated myself with it — its injuries and captivity allowed me to think of it as a fellow being. Nevertheless, after I tossed the dead shark into the water and

watched as a host of small fish hurried to feed off its carcass, I thought
no more about the experience. Pushing the boat into the water, I rowed
to another part of the reef, an area where the depth increased suddenly
but where the water was crystal clear. There, fascinated by the marine organisms that I could see as I leaned over the side of the dinghy, I began
to feel that it was better to study life than to take it; and although in
years to come I would kill quite a lot of sharks, the interest I derived by
watching living things was eventually to turn me into a passive observer.

Engrossed by the submarine world, I did not realize that the boat
was drifting seaward until something crashed violently into the port side,
almost tossing me over the starboard gunwale, after which I ended up on
my back in the bottom of the boat. Before I could recover, the dinghy
was hit again, this time on the starboard quarter, and I heard a loud
scraping sound. Once more I was thrown backward, on this occasion
cracking my head against the after thwart and so taking a little longer to
recover.

As I was about to grab the gunwales with both hands so as to help
myself upright, I suddenly realized that the boat was being attacked by
something large and powerful. Shark, I thought, whipping my hands
away and grabbing instead for the center thwart. Steadying myself as best
I could in the wildly rocking boat, I knelt upright and looked around
me, but beyond a circle of disturbed water, there was nothing to be seen.
I still believed that a large shark had attacked the boat and decided to
make for the reef. I realized that the boat had drifted more than a mile
from land. I had not noted this earlier because, although the depth had
increased measurably, the water was so clear that I had still been able to
see the bottom. Apprehensive, and anxious to get back, I thrust the oars
into the locks and prepared to make for shore.

Just as the dinghy was facing in the right direction, the starboard oar
was struck with such force that it was pulled out of my hand. Fortunately, it did not jump out of the U-shaped oarlock, or else I would have
lost it. As it was, I managed to get hold of it again while at the same time
shipping the port oar, bringing it inboard. Thus engaged, I could feel an
enormous pull on the other oar, then the handle end began to shake vio-

lently. Using both hands, I lifted the oar clear of its lock and began to pull it, at first without gaining so much as an inch. Because whatever held the blade was pulling downward, I was forced to lean in the opposite direction and so was unable to see my attacker, although by now I was convinced that I was dealing with a large shark. Perhaps half a minute later, the oar was suddenly released, causing me to fall one more time. But I had rescued the blade!

I managed to kneel on the bottom, supporting myself by holding onto the seat. Now I could see, but the shark had dived. After scanning the surface and looking downward without detecting anything larger than a couple of black-tips, I began to hope that my unwelcome visitor had not enjoyed the taste of wood and had elected to seek more appetizing prey elsewhere. Nevertheless, I did not immediately try to row for shore, feeling that by disturbing the water, I might encourage the invisible brute to come charging back. Some minutes later, as the rocking subsided, I perched myself on the center seat and examined the oar. The blade was deeply gashed; a piece about three inches long by two wide, but of irregular shape, had been bitten away. Then I saw half a shark's tooth embedded in the wood. I busied myself digging out the fragment, which was more than an inch long and shaped like the tip of a dagger. Its edges were smooth and its point was exceptionally sharp. I had not seen such a tooth before.

I spent about ten minutes removing the fragment from the wood and studying it. At the end of this time, as the boat had not again been struck and I was unable to spot further signs of my assailant, I thought it best to make for shore, for I was drifting farther out to sea.

Leaving the damaged oar in the boat and using the spare blade in its place, I started rowing, but I don't think I had gained more than 100 yards when the shark rose swiftly and charged at the starboard oar. Fortunately, I had just completed a stroke and was lifting the blade clear of the water when the selachian attacked, missing the oar but hitting the side of the boat, once more upsetting me and landing me in the bottom, my arms outstretched and the blade pointing skyward. Remaining prone, I brought the oars on board and waited for further developments, feeling very vulnerable.

This time I had caught a glimpse of the attacker. It was, indeed, a large shark, a two-toned fish, the back a metallic blue, the undersides milk white. I had not seen much else except the dorsal fin, which was short and rounded on top. My initial impression was that the shark was as long as my boat, but since I had not seen the tail, I was not sure of that estimate.

While I considered such things, I remained lying on the bottom, thinking that the shark might well have been attracted by my presence and thus struck at my craft and oars in an effort to reach me. Then, as I was about to sit up, the beast charged again, hitting the port quarter and tossing the bows clear of the water. By now I was seriously worried. The shark, whatever its kind, did not appear ready to give up, and I was afraid that if it kept hitting the wooden hull as it had just done, it might in the end sink my vessel. And I had no desire to find myself in the water with that aggressive creature! Besides, I was continuing to drift, and the farther I was pushed away from shore, the longer it would take to return and the more opportunity my attacker would have to finish the job.

When the boat stopped rocking, I got on the seat, then changed my mind, deciding to use one oar rather like a lever, placing the blade flat against the center of the transom and using the latter as a fulcrum, in this way pulling the oar handle inward each time the blade entered the water, thus attaining some way. I found that although the boat did move forward, I could not keep it pointed toward shore. Now I tried another gambit. Sitting facing the bows, I used one oar as a paddle, alternately stroking to port and to starboard. This was better. I began to move ahead and managed to keep the bows aimed at Sharm el Sheikh, although my speed was little better than a slow crawl.

After paddling awkwardly for some 20 minutes without having attracted the shark's interest, I decided I would again try to row in a conventional way, for my arms were getting tired and my shoulders were feeling the strain. Switching to the center seat, my back to shore, I began rowing as hard as I could, but after a few minutes the shark appeared once more.

I saw its fin before it reached the boat and was able to ship the oars and grab the seat to steady myself for the expected impact. But the shark submerged and swam under my craft, surfacing again about 30 feet to starboard, from where it began to circle me at a distance of 20 feet.

Long ago, I had learned to master my fear by turning it into controlled anger. This I now did by thinking offensively, telling myself that should the shark succeed in destroying my craft and, therefore, being able to kill me, I would make sure it would pay for the deed with its own life. Having goaded myself into an aggressive mood, I began to analyze the situation.

The shark was determined to kill me. It was large, probably 11 or 12 feet long, and would have weighed 1,000 pounds or more. Studying it as it continued to circle, I noted that its body was thick across the back and deep on the undersides. It had a half-moon-shaped tail, and because it was swimming with its head partly raised to inspect me at leisure, I saw its exceptionally large black eyes. Now and then one of those devil orbs became fixed on me; I glared back, telegraphing my anger, and reviewed my options: I had left the lily iron on shore, but I had brought the smaller hand harpoon. This was too short a weapon to use from the boat; it would only increase the selachian's aggressiveness. But if I was tossed into the water, it would at least give me a chance to fatally wound my attacker. The big fish would undoubtedly kill me and devour parts of my body, but it would eventually die from its wounds.

I had just reached that unpleasant conclusion when I remembered the Thompson! Wrapped in canvas, it reposed in one of the forward lockers with eight fully loaded magazines, each containing twenty .45-caliber cartridges.

Feeling enormous relief that I had at last remembered it, I began crawling forward cautiously. The shark attacked again, hitting the stern this time, a glancing blow that drove the boat forward and propelled me toward the locker. Moments later I had thrust a magazine into the Thompson, cocked the firing mechanism and glanced about me, looking for the shark. It had dived!

I have never been a superstitious person, but at this point I was beginning to think that my attacker was some kind of incubus, an evil and supernatural being who could read my mind and knew that if I was prevented from using the oars I would drift far out to sea and be totally helpless, sooner or later becoming easy prey.

Coincidental with these thoughts, the shark surfaced some 50 feet in front of the bows. It was too far to try for a brain shot, so I thrust an oar into the water and waggled it in what I hoped was an attractive way. My ruse worked. The shark sped straight for the boat. Shipping the oar quickly and grabbing the Thompson, I waited until the selachian was 15 feet away, then fired a short burst into its head.

The shark lunged upward, shaking its massive head from side to side and at the same time thrashing with its tail. It began to slide downward, still shaking, but more slowly.

I became mesmerized as the great body began to twitch and seeing its blood staining the water, masses of it, a slowly widening circle of red that soon obscured the shark.

I grabbed the oars and rowed toward the dead fish. I had intended to harpoon it and tow it to shore, but when I looked down just before the water became obscured by the blood, I saw about a dozen large, shadowy shapes coming upward. There was no mistaking those outlines, despite the fact that their physical details were indistinct. The grotesque, T-shaped pates identified them as hammerheads, of which there are nine known species, all voracious hunters that prey on fish, other sharks and occasionally on humans. The surface commotion, the scent of blood and no doubt the concussive reports of the Thompson had attracted the school.

The shark I had killed was sinking slowly. I conquered the urge to make for shore and decided to watch the hammerheads, for I had been offered a wonderful opportunity to observe the feeding techniques of a species I had never seen before.

Sitting in the boat behind the trail of blood, which was traveling seaward, I had a relatively good view of the underwater scene. When the dead shark had sunk about 15 feet, the hammerheads accelerated their pace, aiming their astonishing heads toward the surface as they formed an irregular circle. Soon I was able to note that the wide, flat noses (if one can apply such a term to the leading edge of a hammerhead's body) were scalloped, a characteristic that later allowed me to identify them as *Sphyrna lewini*, or, as the wavy snouts suggest, scalloped hammerheads — a species that attains a length of between 12 and 14 feet and that may weigh up to 1,000 pounds. Found mostly in tropical waters around the world year-round, they are also known to frequent the east and west coasts of the United States during the height of summer, especially in North and South Carolina and the Gulf of Mexico, where they are relatively abundant during the warm season.

Two of the leading hammerheads made a sudden dash for the dead shark. One struck at the bleeding head, the other grasped the underside, appearing to disembowel the corpse. In seconds, there was a rush of activity as 16 voracious hammerheads ripped and tore at my erstwhile attacker, each shark boring straight in, opening the upper and lower jaws, clamping down on meat and shaking their heads rapidly from side to side to remove great chunks of flesh. Within a minute or two, I could hardly see what was happening because of blood and bits of meat. The remains of the dead shark were sinking more rapidly, and the gang of hammerheads followed it downward. At this stage, it seemed prudent to leave the area.

As far as I am aware, there is no evidence to suggest that hammerheads are in the habit of attacking boats, but at the time, remembering all too clearly the way in which the dead shark had behaved, I was in no mood to take any more chances. Rowing steadily while being careful not to create undue splashing, it took me somewhat longer than an hour to reach the shore. By then, it was almost evening. I was hungry, tired and still rather intimidated by my experience, but remembering the dictum which says that if you are thrown off a horse, you had better climb on it immediately afterward or risk developing a fear of riding, I took up the shark club and dived in a relatively shallow part of the reef, going down about 30 feet and, clinging to the coral, remaining quietly submerged while trying to see what was going on around me in the now almost darkened water. Need for air drove me to the surface, and if my heart was beating a little faster than normal as I clambered out of the sea, I knew that my recent altercation with the big shark would not have the power to make me fearful of the species. I did, however, decide to be more cautious in the future, knowing that it is dangerous for a lone diver to venture too rashly into the world of the sharks.

During the remainder of my short stay in Sharm el Sheikh, I devoted most of my attention to the reef and the many different fish and fishlike organisms that live there. Diving several times daily, I collected small specimens for leisurely examination on the surface, occasionally going down merely to observe the life of the reef and remaining immobile for the short time that each descent permitted.

In this way, I spent another week at Sharm el Sheikh. Although I had six more days of leave at the end of that time, when a Royal Navy corvette hove-to some 200 yards from shore and its skipper hailed me through a megaphone. Our meeting and conversation resulted in my being offered a free luxury ride to Ismailia, in Egypt. I accepted the invitation with alacrity, for, in truth, I had been a bit worried about getting back to my unit without overstaying my leave, since I had not the vaguest idea when I would be able to pick up an Egypt-army convoy at Elat, an outpost of civilization I had planned to reach by hitching another ride in an Arab fishing boat.

In any event, I returned to my tank unit on time and was once more absorbed by the war, not realizing that seven years would have to pass before I was again able to study sharks.

THE TIGER SHARK INHABITS TROPICAL AND
SUBTROPICAL OCEANS, GROWING UP TO 30 FEET LONG
AND WEIGHING AS MUCH AS 1,200 POUNDS.

# Chapter 4

A CLOSELY as I could determine from the old Spanish charts and a gimbaled compass that had seen much better days, we were some 300 miles off the Moroccan coast, probably in a line with, and nor-nor-east of, Casablanca when the sea began to moderate. The wind slowed from what I judged had been Force Six on the Beaufort scale to a far more comfortable Force Three, and wave height fluctuated between three and five feet. I felt I could now safely begin to dissect the 14-foot blue shark, a female that we had hooked at 5:00 a.m. and which by two o'clock had been lying on the afterdeck for nine hours.

Exposed for so long to the summer heat, even in the absence of continuous sunlight, I knew that the task of opening and examining the blue was going to be accompanied by a distinctly unpleasant odor. So did the captain and his two crew members, who became exceptionally busy tidying up the moment I went to get my dissecting tools!

Four days earlier, I had boarded the felucca, a 33-foot Mediterranean-type sailing vessel that was equipped with an old but well-maintained diesel motor. The *Mi Querida* (*My Beloved*) was the pride and joy of Pedro Roquena, an ex-lieutenant in the defunct Spanish Republican navy whose youngest brother, José, had been a close school friend of mine in Barcelona, the city in which I grew up until my late teens. In the early 1930s, Pedro had often taken me along when he and José went on

fishing trips and, because of my friendship with the youngest member of
the family, I used to spend many hours at the Roquena home. On July
18, 1936, the Spanish Civil War changed all that. Each of us went our
own way. I was never to see José again, for he was killed at a place called
Albacete in 1937, fighting against the fascist forces. He was 16 years old
at the time. But I was not to learn of my friend's death until 12 years
later when, quite by accident, I ran into Pedro in Gibraltar in late June
of 1949.

Now, in early July of that same year, I was a nominal member of *Mi
Querida*'s crew, having no specific duties but inscribed on the vessel's roll
in order to satisfy official requirements, a circumstance that came about
after Pedro told me that, having been dismissed from the navy after
Franco's forces won the war and being unable to find other employment
because he had supported the Republican government, he had taken to
commercial fishing, his seamanship and knowledge of the ocean combining to make him successful. As navigator under an aging captain and
sailing out of Malaga, Pedro had slowly saved money, augmenting his
wages by "moonlighting" as navigator for a smuggler's launch that plied
between Tangiers and Malaga, carrying such contraband as scented
soaps, American and British cigarettes, nylon stockings and other luxu-
ries that could only be had in postwar Spain through a vigorous black
market. In time, Pedro was able to buy his own felucca, the *Mi Querida*,
and gave up the night runs from Tangiers in order to devote himself to
the catching of swordfish and sharks — the first for the fish market, the
second for their livers, from which vitamins A and D were processed,
and for their dried fins, purchased by Asian buyers for shark-fin soup.

At the time of my accidental meeting with Pedro, I was taking a long
holiday in the land of my youth, a country I had not seen since my
escape into France via the Pyrenean Mountains in the winter of 1938. It
happened that I was visiting friends in Gibraltar and had gone for a stroll
down to the Waterport market to watch the Spanish fishing boats unload
their catches (Gibraltar paid better prices for the fish, in much sought-
after Gibraltarian pounds sterling) when Roquena's boat came in. By that
evening, I had decided to spend some time on *Mi Querida*, paying my

friend a nominal per diem fee for my keep and helping with chores as I was needed. In exchange, I got to fish for sharks, study them, cut them open, weigh them and help store their livers in large metal drums. Our home port was Algeciras, a small town of Moorish origin that nestles on the west side of the Bay of Gibraltar right opposite the British rock fortress from which the bay takes its name.

Four days after my agreement with Pedro, we left Algeciras, at first using the motor to get out of the bay, then, entering the Strait of Gibraltar and hoisting the lateen and jib sails, the two-masted barque caught the Mediterranean Levanter wind that funnels through the narrow strait that divides Spain and North Africa. Our course was westerly, for we were heading to a point 200 miles off Casablanca where Pedro had often caught giant swordfish, some of them 18 feet long and therefore fetching a good price.

As we had come abreast of Gibraltar's Europa Point, and while the crew was hoisting sail as we entered the strait, I trained my field glasses on The Rock's southernmost feature, a sharp, raised spur of land from which, traditionally, the British fired a gun to mark the noon hour, an event that is just one of the ties to the colorful history of the great rock massif that has for centuries guarded the entrance to the Mediterranean Sea. The Moors called it Jabal Tariq, which corrupted by Spaniard and Englishman, became Gibraltar. Europa Point itself was known to the Romans as Heracles, one of the two Pillars of Hercules, the companion to which lies across the strait at Ceuta and was known as Meqart. Legend has it that Hercules was responsible for separating Europe and Africa when, one hand on each pillar, he pushed the two continents apart.

Making about seven knots, it took us somewhat more than five hours to enter the Atlantic, passing Cape Spartel and Tangiers to port on a west-nor-west bearing, heading for an area of ocean below which the jagged submarine mountains of the Azores Rise thrust their heads upward between 9,000 and 15,000 feet below the surface. Somewhere in those deeps, said Pedro, the big swordfish hunted; so did large sharks. En route to these fishing grounds, one of *Mi Querida*'s crewmen, Alfredo, busied himself trolling for mackerel to use as swordfish and shark bait.

These sleek, beautiful fish are related to the tunnies, albacores and boni-tos, all of which are so streamlined that, according to early nautical engineers, their body shapes are "perfect for passing through the water with the least amount of resistance." Mackerel are found in most seas, including the Pacific, Mediterranean and Atlantic, but the latter species, the kind Alfredo was catching, are characterized by having no air bladder, a physical distinction that allows them to swim rapidly between surface and bottom, even in great depths, without ill effects.

Using large shrimp spiked on a series of hooks that were attached by short lines to a long steel leader, Alfredo let down 100 meters (about 54 fathoms) of heavily weighted line, periodically winching this inboard by means of a small auxiliary engine. Each time the line was retrieved, from three to as many as nine beautifully marked mackerel came up with it, all between 18 and 20 inches long and weighing two to four pounds.

When several dozen of these fish were put into ice in the forward hold, Alfredo, his companion, Manolo, and I began to prepare swordfish baits. This was done by tying one mackerel to the shank of a large hook that had itself been tied to a flat piece of board three-quarters of an inch thick, some three inches wide and about 16 inches long; the hook was attached to a six-foot steel leader, which in turn was secured to the line by a heavy swivel fastener. Some 20 feet from the bait, large balls of lead weights were secured. Depth was attained in accordance with the number of weights attached to the line, while the bait itself, made slightly buoyant by the piece of board, drifted behind the lead, swivelling and undulating as it was towed.

After a dozen or so swordfish baits were prepared and returned to the ice, we prepared shark baits, in this case using enormous hooks that were fixed to three-meter-long chains, "leaders" that would not be abraded by a shark's denticles or cut by a selachian's sharp teeth. A large swivel attached to the last link of each chain would later be secured to the heavy line that filled the enormous drum of a stern-mounted power winch, also operated by the auxiliary engine. On this drum, Pedro explained, 750 meters of line was wound, almost 400 fathoms (2,400 feet). A number of coils of the same line, each containing 100 meters (54 fathoms), hung near the winch. These were for us in the event that deeper fishing was required, in which case, one end would be attached to the steel or chain leader and the other to the winch line before the bait was put over the side. Swordfish run deep at certain times, especially during the torrid heat of a North African day, so with his spare lines, Pedro could put the bait down to 1,000 meters, or almost 600 fathoms.

Unlike the more elaborate swordfish baits, a shark hook was dressed with three mackerel, each fish hooked by the head, then put back on ice, chain and all.

"You have to keep the mackerel fresh," Pedro explained. "Then, just before we put the bait over, we punch a hole in the intestinal cavity. Not a big hole, more like a puncture. That way, the mackerel juices leak out slowly and leave a nice trail in the water. Sharks really go after fish juices."

Since I had never used this system, I took his word, for even though we had not yet started fishing, my friend was efficient and knowledgeable, his old but excellent equipment and his house in Algeciras attesting to his success as a commercial fisherman.

It took us almost two days to reach Pedro's fishing grounds, but once there, a swordfish bait was put over the side almost immediately. It was late evening, but from now on, two men remained on duty all the time, relieved every two hours by the others. My addition to the crew made it possible for each of us to sleep two hours out of four instead of one hour out of three, which was the rule for the regular three-man crew. Of course, if a fish was hooked, everybody turned up.

Nothing, however, took the bait that first night, but shortly before eleven o'clock the next morning, with some 80 fathoms of line out, we got a heavy strike. I had never fished swordfish before, so, having nothing to do, I stationed myself at the stern and watched the line stretch, hearing the hiss it made as it traveled through the water, despite the sound of the engine, and seeing the spray fly off the wet cord. For a time, whatever had become hooked down there made zigzag runs, veering sharply to port, then swinging back as sharply to starboard, the swinging of the line altering in tempo with each wild run. Then the fish

put on more speed as it ran toward the boat. The line went slack despite
the accelerated pace of the winch, which, geared for just such a contin-
gency, was quickly put into fast drive. The fish, nevertheless, gained;
then it dived. Pedro immediately put the winch into free drive, and the
line peeled off the drum at a great rate. But as suddenly as the captive
had dived, it rose again, dramatically slowing the line's momentum.

Pedro, watching from his place beside the winch, forecast the next
move.

"It's going to start swinging again!" he yelled, hand on the lever that
would put the drum into reverse drive.

Perhaps a minute later, before the winch had time to do more than
pick up half the slack, the fish angled to starboard and the line went bar-
taut again. But now the captive appeared to be tiring; the line did not
hiss as loudly as before, and the winch kept reeling it in at a good rate.

Events continued in the same way for perhaps half an hour; alternately the fish gained some line, then lost it again. It dived, rose,
zigzagged, swam toward the boat and repeated its previous maneuvers.
Then, with startling suddenness, it burst out of the water — a long,
sleek, *enormous* fish, gleaming silver and black, its long lethal sword
slashing in the air as the unfortunate creature sought to shed the hook by
shaking its head violently. The entire fish cleared the water; its muscled
body contorted, becoming a wide U; then, with a great splash, it entered
the ocean again, dived, but not too steeply, and charged the boat.

Pedro immediately accelerated the engine while Alfredo, at the
wheel, turned to port. Manolo picked up a long harpoonlike spear and
went to stand by the stern rail. As Pedro worked the winch, he told me
that the fish might well seek to ram its sword into the felucca, a not-
infrequent occurrence. Pedro's concern was not so much for the boat,
which could withstand such a charge, but for the sword, which could
either become embedded in the wooden hull and snap or would remain
stuck, necessitating the killing of the fish while it was still submerged
and, afterward, the need to go over the side with a saw to cut the sword
free, leaving its tip stuck in the wood to be removed in port. Because the
sword had a ready market in bazaars in Spain and North Africa, Pedro

was anxious to avoid the charge. He and Alfredo, working as a team, thwarted the furious fish. Soon afterward, exhausted, the great, valiant animal was brought close to the side. Manolo, who had exchanged the long spear for a more conventional lily iron, plunged the weapon deep into the body of the fish, whereupon the huge animal contorted violently and sought to dive again. But now, secured by the hook as well as by the harpoon head, the swordfish could not escape. It was inexorably drawn toward the boat, then lifted out of the water by the stern hoist until the violently struggling fish was brought against the side almost level with the deck rail. Manolo, who had now retrieved the discarded harpoon, leaned over and stabbed the captive through the brain.

My feelings were mixed as I stood nearby and watched the throes of that magnificent sea creature. I was excited by the prospect of being able to examine the swordfish, a species I had never seen until now; but as the contorting animal was hoisted over the rail then lowered to the deck, where it lay jerking feebly as the death tremors caused its body to quiver spasmodically, it seemed to me that its killing was amoral, a predatory act that the fish would commit solely in order to eat. Pedro, on the other hand, was merchandising death; and although I realized he was doing so in order to provide for his family as well as for Alfredo and Manolo, I could not help thinking that the business of killing for gain rather than personal consumption was contrary to the laws of nature. Then, too, it struck me that without the mechanical means at our disposal, none of us, either singly or collectively, could match the prowess of that great fish which, in its own domain, could so easily evade us or kill us.

I continued to watch the swordfish, noticing that its gorgeous metallic blue color was beginning to fade as the large, round, black eyes became opaque and lusterless. A moment later, the animal was dead. And my own involvement with its killing made me remorseful and ashamed. Did I have the right to participate in such slaughter?

I have asked myself that question a number of times since that day. Although I can justify my involvement with the merchants of death on the grounds that I am seeking knowledge, I often feel that this excuse is prompted more by sophistry than by reality, that my cortex could always find reasons why death was acceptable if it were commissioned in the cause of science. On the other hand, the deeper part of my mind, and especially that innermost part of my being, inevitably rejects the need to kill in order to learn.

Nowadays, I rarely place myself in the center of such an argument, preferring to observe quietly and over the long haul rather than to participate in any kind of killing, even as a spectator. But my past involvements still gnaw at my conscience.

Perhaps Pedro read something about my feelings in the way I stood watching the fish, or it may be that he had similar feelings. In any event, the remark he made in Spanish reflected pity: *"Que bonito es! Lástima que uno tenga que matarlo."* ("How pretty it is! It's a pity one must kill it.")

The swordfish measured 21 feet from tail fork to sword tip; the body itself was 16 feet 4 inches. It was thicker than a man's waist at the dorsal-ventral midsection.

I watched as Alfredo and Manolo expertly gutted it, cut off its sword and fins and, leaving the head attached, hoisted it into the ice-filled midships hold. I examined its internal organs, finding in its stomach three mackerel in various stages of digestive decomposition and a bizarre fish that was 37 inches long but as thin as an eel. This specimen was in relatively good condition, suggesting that it had been recently ingested, although parts of its pencillike body were badly torn. The head of this creature was narrow, the snout pointed, the lower jaw protruding slightly beyond the upper. Its mouth was filled with fangs that were almost half an inch long and finely pointed, and its eyes were exceptionally large and protruding outward from the sides of the head. My reference book identified it as a frostfish (*Benthodesmus atlanticus*), an animal of the deeps, although the absence of light organs, the large well-developed eyes and the fact that the swordfish we had hooked at about the 200-fathom zone had swallowed it not long before its own capture, all suggested that the frostfish may not dwell below the 1,700-foot, utterly dark depths.

BY MIDAFTERNOON of that same day, the *Mi Querida*'s crew had taken two more swordfish, one with a body length of 9 feet, the second measuring 17 feet overall, the body being 13 feet 8 inches long.

In all, and according to Pedro's scales, the combined weight of the three great fish totalled 1,480 kilograms, or 3,263 pounds! I seem to recall that Pedro expected to get between 2.80 and 3.25 pesetas per pound of swordfish, whole weight, which translated to at least 4,000 pesetas for the three fish. This was considered an excellent catch and a greedy skipper might well have continued fishing for more of the same. But the cold-storage hold wasn't very roomy and the three fish took up a lot of its space, so my friend decided that now was the time to go after sharks, a task to which he allotted two more days, after which the *Mi Querida* would turn about and make for Gibraltar, for the fresher his catch, the more Pedro would make at the Waterport market.

After an early supper of fried mackerel, sweet peppers, tomatoes and boiled beans seasoned with raw garlic, the first shark bait was put over the side and allowed to drop 100 meters; but by dark, nothing had sought the bunched mackerel. The bait was then changed and two large carbide-fueled lights were hung over the stern, each having an enormous, coolie hat-type of metal shade, so that most of the light was spread over the water. This was essential illumination in the event that a shark became hooked, for to try to subdue one of these fish in the dark was a difficult and dangerous job.

For me, the lights served another purpose: they attracted a variety of fish to our stern. Because we were using sail, only a slow, smooth wake disturbed the surface; this allowed me to see clearly. Staring into the water, I noted literally hundreds of fish and was fascinated by the phosphorescent properties of many of the smaller ones and of the vast horde of planktonic organisms. Outside the focus of our lanterns, the ocean winked and sparkled, especially where the wake roiled the surface, as millions of tiny green lights flashed on and off. At one point, what I took to be a large school of squid ghosted swiftly under the surface, each flowing green, the combined, subdued lights forming a large luminescent cloud over a wide area of the water. It was hard to tell just how deep the squid were; I guessed at between three and four fathoms, but I felt the sight was interesting enough to mention to Pedro, who was at the wheel.

The news galvanized our captain into action. Yelling at Alfredo to take the wheel and at Manolo to raise the shark bait, Pedro came to the stern just in time to witness the passing cloud of green, which appeared to be heading to starboard. He shouted a change of course to Alfredo as he started the engine, meanwhile telling Manolo to bring the bait up to ten meters from the surface (slightly more than six fathoms).

Responding to the engine, the felucca accelerated her pace while Alfredo set a course intended to intercept the luminous cloud. Pedro, coming to stand beside me at the stern, explained the reason for the recent activity, telling me that sharks feed on schools of squid and, provided we could intercept this one, we might well get a strike. We did. It happened just moments after Pedro finished speaking and while we were yet some distance from the faint light that marked the contours of the massed squid.

After the first hard jerk on the line, it seemed that either the fish had not been hooked or it was a small one. For some moments, we weren't even sure that it was a shark that had struck the bait. But then the captive began to fight, pulling line off the drum at a great rate before Alfredo could slow the momentum by gradually increasing the drag and ultimately stopping the line altogether. At this stage, the shark — and we were now certain it was a selachian — began to saw on the line much as the swordfish had done, turning to port, then reversing itself and making for starboard. It did this about half a dozen times before trying to dive. But unlike fishing with a rod and relatively light tackle, which requires an angler to play the fish, commercial fishermen use heavy line so they can bring in the catch as quickly as possible. The shark, therefore, could not dive deeply. Checked, it hesitated, evidently swimming slowly in the same direction as the felucca was traveling. Alfredo began to retrieve line. Responding to the tug, the shark increased speed without altering course, but as Alfredo put the winch in higher gear to gather more slack, the fish burst out of the water. We could see the great shark in outline as it contorted in the air at the extreme range of our lights.

"*Isurus,*" Pedro said excitedly, giving the mako its Latin name, an instant identification based on the shark's fighting qualities and particularly by the way it leaped out of the water.

When the mako fell back on the surface, it made a resounding splash, but it soon came up again, essaying an even more prodigious jump and shaking itself frantically as it tried to shed the hook.

This was the same kind of shark that had attacked my boat off Sharm el Sheikh! Pedro had caught a large number of them and, as he told me later, every mako he had captured put up an enormous fight, during which it repeatedly leaped out of the water, as the present captive kept doing, until it was finally subdued 40 minutes after it took the hook.

When the mako was close to the stern and thus in full light, I found myself staring at a massive shark. Apart from its length — eleven feet four inches — it was of large girth, a deep metallic blue on the back and partway down the sides and glaringly white on the undersides; a milky hue that extended to the snout and right around the mouth was filled with long, slim and sharply pointed teeth.

Breaking off my observations to help Pedro attach a line over the moon-shaped tail, and while leaning far out, holding the rail with one hand, I was only about three feet above the mako, which was secured by the line and also by the lily iron that Manolo had driven into its body. The big shark was still fighting, but its actions were slower; even so, it was hard to slip the noose around the lashing tail. Leaning even farther out, just as we at last managed to lasso the caudal fin, I found myself looking at the mako's undersides, noting that the shark was a female. As I stared, I was startled by a series of quick contractions that convulsed the stomach. Almost immediately after, I saw a small shark being born, a pup about 18 inches long. This was followed in quick succession by three more, each appearance preceded by the contractions of the mother. As a pup emerged, it quickly swam downward and disappeared, obviously quite well able to survive despite the abrupt circumstances that had preceded its birth. Busy for a time helping to bring the mako inboard, I merely assumed that the birth time of the pups had coincided with the mother's capture and that her exertions had slightly accelerated delivery of the young. But later, discussing the event with Pedro, I was surprised to learn that every pregnant female mako he had caught aborted her young before she could be subdued and hauled on deck, in some cases long before the pups were ready to be born, in others, as I had observed, while the young sharks were sufficiently developed to survive. Much later, these findings were confirmed by a number of other investigators, accounting for the fact that, although it is known that mako sharks are ovoviviparous, hatching inside the mother in their own self-contained eggs, the female's practice of aborting during capture prevents full understanding of this shark's reproductive biology.

Pedro did not normally weigh the sharks that he caught, but because the flesh of mako is much appreciated in Europe and elsewhere, we hoisted the female — after making absolutely sure that she was dead! — and found that an hour after capture she weighed 1,008 pounds. Her huge liver, weighed separately for my own information, tipped the scales at 238 pounds — almost 24 percent of the shark's total weight — a great oily organ with long lobes that yield a large amount of oil and vitamins.

Two species of mako sharks are presently recognized, the shortfin (*Isurus oxyrinchus*), like the big female we caught that night, and the longfin (*Isurus paucus*). The shortfin is at home in warm and warm-temperate waters throughout the oceans of the world; it is distinguished from its relative by having somewhat short pectoral fins. The largest-known specimen recorded to date was 12½ feet long and weighed 1,250 pounds, but sightings by reliable observers suggest that there are short-fins in the ocean that are longer and heavier than the present record holder. Females of this species are usually larger than the males, maturing when they are about eight and a half feet long and weighing between 300 and 500 pounds, whereas males mature when they are about six feet long and have attained a weight of 150 to 350 pounds.

The shortfin mako is massive enough to be confused for a white shark, especially in view of its light underparts, yet anybody who has seen a great white at close quarters can never mistake this formidable fish for any other kind of selachian. "Whitey" is more streamlined, his nose, or snout, is straight instead of being slightly upturned like the shortfin's, and his way of moving, quietly and fluidly, is unmistakable. Nevertheless, the five species recognized as belonging to the Lamnidae family are all big, formidable predators.

The longfin mako, as its common name implies, has very large pectoral fins and a taller, more pointed first dorsal fin; its color is blue-black on the upper part of its body and a dusky gray on the undersides. It is believed to grow larger than its near relative, the record standing at 13 feet 7 inches. Both the shortfin and longfin have large eyes, an indication that these fish spend at least part of their time in deep waters, but they nevertheless come close to the surface on occasion, especially at night.

After our big shark had been measured and weighed that night, I opened her up, first examining the two womblike sacks in which the eggs of ovoviviparous sharks develop. They were empty, and since it is believed that eight to ten pups are common in this species, I could only presume that she had aborted most of her young before being brought up short against our boat. Interestingly, and although I was unaware of it at the time, this shark has the ability to maintain its muscle temperature 7° to 10°C higher than the surrounding water — a characteristic shared by other large selachians.

The remaining two members of the Lamnidae family are the salmon shark (*Lamna ditropis*) and the porbeagle shark (*Lamna nasus*).

FOR TWO HOURS after we had caught the mako, we lost several shark baits to smaller fish of unknown kinds but failed to hook into any shark. Our luck changed around 11:00 p.m., however, when a small smooth hammerhead (*Sphyrna zygaena*) swallowed the hook. This species, also found in warm-temperate waters throughout the world, gets its name from the fact that, unlike most other hammerheads, it lacks an indentation in the center of the leading edge of its head. Like most of the hammerheads — six species comprise this family, the Sphyrnidae — the smooth hammerhead is a voracious fish that is considered dangerous to divers and swimmers. It is known to reach a length of 13 feet and to weigh more than 1,000 pounds, but the five-foot two-inch specimen that we took from the water in something under ten minutes did not seem to have much fight left in it by the time it reached our stern, although it did quite a lot of running, turning and surface flopping during the short time it fought the hook and line. Only minutes later, as I was examining the brain-speared fish, which was a male, Manolo announced a second strike. This time the shark was bigger; another male hammerhead of the same species, but eight feet ten inches long and very active, requiring almost an hour to subdue. The small shark weighed 136 pounds and the larger one weighed 308 pounds. Both had good livers, which were removed and placed in the barrel that already contained the huge liver of the mako.

For the remainder of that night, while we continued to stand watch two hours on and two off, our bait remained untouched, but just before 5:00 a.m., a big blue shark struck hard, fought vigorously for a short time, then came in fairly quietly — a behavior not uncharacteristic of this species. By 6:30 that morning, we had weighed the blue, which scaled 491 pounds, and were preparing to open her before having our breakfast when the wind freshened and heavy clouds began to fill the skies. The three Spaniards recognized the signs, telling me that a storm was coming soon; because of this, we elected to eat first and postpone the butcher work until later. But our coffee and bread repast was not quite finished when a "strong breeze" began to build the seas, the waves cresting at about eight feet and making life aboard the *Mi Querida* a far from pleasant experience. Pedro took the wheel while Alfredo, Manolo and I secured the boat and lowered the jib and foresail as our captain prepared to run before the wind.

It was not a bad storm but it caused us to veer sharply off course and to put more distance between ourselves and the coast than we had planned on. So when the weather abated, Pedro decided to turn about and make for Gibraltar — a journey that at an average of seven knots would take at least 42 hours, provided we did not run into more heavy weather. My friend's sudden decision to go back stemmed from the fact that although at least half the ice remained in the midships hold, the summer heat in those latitudes is intense and Pedro was afraid that if we ran into another patch of bad weather and got pushed farther off course, his catch might spoil.

While the crew attended to our vessel, I busied myself with the odorous shark, opening the stomach and finding that she was carrying 69 pups, all dead now, but seemingly not fully developed. Beyond this, the blue had eaten a variety of fish, including a number of mackerel, but most of her stomach contents were in an advanced stage of digestion and could not be identified. Death and long hours of exposure on deck had dulled the shark's beautiful blue color, but nothing could alter the svelte lines of this beautiful fish. Long-nosed, with finely pointed snout and very long pectoral fins, the body of these sharks tapers gracefully to a heavy caudal, or tail, fin, the upper lobe being wider and at least twice as long as the lower lobe.

Blue sharks have a worldwide distribution within tropical, subtropical and temperate waters where the temperature ranges between 10° and 20°C (60° and 68°F); and although recent literature states that they are usually found at depths greater than 100 fathoms and that they rarely venture near land, hard evidence gathered by the United States National Marine Fisheries Service in 1972 shows that blues feed at all water depths. This is something that those of us who have actually seen blue sharks traveling in relatively shallow waters, as Nick and I did off the Sinai coast, did not need to be told.

That these sharks are great travelers has long been surmised, but in more recent years, and again because of work done by the U.S. National Marine Fisheries Service, it is now confirmed that blues commonly travel great distances. The present record was set by one member of this species that was caught and tagged off Montauk, New York, and recaptured nine months later off the coast of Liberia, Africa, at latitude 1° 34' N and longitude 21° 07' W, within only some 90 miles of the equator, having covered a *straight-line* distance of 3,630 miles (5,842 kilometers). Another member of this species, tagged off New York, traveled 3,150 miles (5,069 kilometers) in 483 days. But these are just the records; recovered tags show that long journeys are commonly made by these sharks.

The blue is also distinguished by being probably the most prolific of all the big sharks, producing from 25 to as many as 135 pups after a gestation period that fluctuates between nine months and one year. The newborn sharklets are usually between 16 and 20 inches long, but, of course, not all sibling pups are exactly the same size. The smallest of the pups carried by the female I was dissecting on board the *Mi Querida* was 14⅞ inches long, the largest 20³⁄₁₆ inches long. The species are viviparous: the embryos develop in the mother's twin wombs and take nourishment from her system. This fact makes the large numbers of young quite remarkable from a nutritional standpoint: the mother has to eat enough to sustain herself while nourishing between slightly more than two dozen and slightly less than twelve dozen developing embryos!

This species is known to have participated in attacks on victims of sea disasters. In tests, using dummy human figures in yellow suits and life rafts, blue sharks repeatedly attacked these objects, showing a distinct fascination for yellow. Because of these things, *Prionace glauca* should be regarded as potentially dangerous — as should almost all large sharks — although this species does not appear to be a voracious feeder. Illustrating this, a 132-pound blue, which had eaten the most fish out of a total of 523 blues whose stomachs were examined, had ingested 15 pounds of food consisting of 21 yellowtail flounder, 3 hakes, 1 unidentified fish and some bait. This amount represented 8.8 percent of the shark's total weight. Further studies showed that blue sharks digest their food at a rate of 2.6 pounds per 24 hours, or something in the order of 3 percent of their body weight per day.

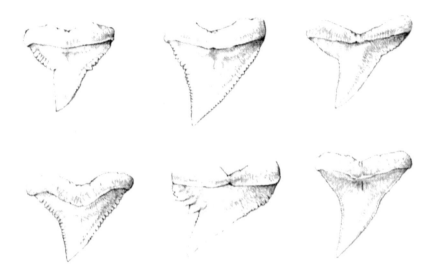

THE TEETH OF SHARKS VARY CONSIDERABLY.
TOP ROW, LEFT TO RIGHT: TIGER, GREAT WHITE, MAKO;
BOTTOM ROW, LEFT TO RIGHT: BULL, SAND, BLUE.

# Chapter 5

I N LATE AUGUST, while we were returning to Pedro Roquena's home port after a five-day trip that had only yielded one medium-sized swordfish and three good-sized makos, Manolo was bitten by a small tiger shark, a fish that was only 39 inches long and which I had caught while using a sea rod.

Characteristically, the tiger, despite its small size, put up a vigorous fight, causing me to play it for more than half an hour before I could get it to the side and earning for me a lot of good-natured banter from the *Mi Querida's* crew, for the little fish had the distinction of being the smallest selachian that we had caught during nearly two months of fishing. Manolo, who hailed from Cadiz and had the typical Andalusian wit, teased constantly, alternately cheering for the shark and then for me, when he would congratulate me for having hooked "such a monstrous fish!"

When the tiger was brought close to the stern, there to lie placidly, Manolo grabbed the rope noose and rashly leaned far over the deck, chuckling about the very dangerous "*tiburon.*" Contemptuously, holding to a stanchion with his left hand, he reached for the shark's tail, intending to slip the noose over it; his hand was only inches from the water. Then it happened. The seemingly exhausted fish burst into action, reversing itself and fastening its jaws on Manolo's arm. Immediately it had secured a grip and it began shaking its head from side to side.

Watching horrified as the blood flowed, I dropped the rod, snatched up the lily iron and rammed it deep into the tiger shark's body, pulling upward on the rope as soon as the shaft disengaged from the head. Manolo and the struggling shark came up simultaneously, and Pedro, who had meanwhile picked up a stunning club, smashed the shark over the head. Now it let go of Manolo's arm.

The young crewman, white beneath his tan and gritting his teeth in pain, held his arm, his left hand pressing the brachial artery at a point just inside the bend of the elbow. The arm was a gory mess; lacerated severely, in three places it showed the bone, and despite the pressure that Manolo was exerting, blood spurted in all directions until Alfredo came running with the first-aid kit and secured a tourniquet above the injury.

We cleaned up the wounds as best we could, applying copious amounts of peroxide before bandaging, while Pedro put the engine at full throttle and conned the *Mi Querida* on course for Tangier, the nearest port offering hospital facilities. Meanwhile, we put the suffering Manolo to bed, but even pain could not entirely banish the Andalusian's wit. As I was about to leave the small cabin, he called out, *"Vaya, ya te dije que ese tiburon era un monstruo!"* ("There, I told you this shark was a monster!")

We were some 35 nautical miles from Cape Spartel at the southern entrance to the Mediterranean. Tangier is located just inside the Strait of Gibraltar, in the bay formed by the cape, perhaps four miles from the salient. Nevertheless, it took us slightly more than four hours to enter harbor and another half an hour to get Manolo into hospital, where doctors had to use 63 stitches to close up his wounds. If any of us needed to be convinced of the awesome power of a shark's teeth and jaws, the damage inflicted on Manolo's arm by that little shark would have done that! Pedro, while greatly concerned for the young man, was annoyed with him for being so careless and allowing himself to be misled by the tiger shark's small size and deceptive tranquility.

In any event, Manolo spent only two days in hospital and was to recover fully. I last saw him during his early days of convalescence when I went to say goodbye to Pedro and his crew. His arm still bandaged,

Manolo told me he would never forget me because of his injury. I replied that I would never forget *him*, especially when I had to handle a live shark.

THE TIGER SHARK (*Galeocerdo cuvieri*) belongs to one of the largest shark families, the Carcharhinidae, which comprises some 60 known species to date; all are voracious feeders, and therefore extremely active when hungry, although the majority are not known to be a threat to humans. A few species including the tiger, however, known as requiem sharks, have proved themselves to be dangerous to swimmers, divers and sea-disaster victims (the term "requiem" has been taken from the Mass of the same name celebrated for the repose of the dead by the Roman Catholic Church).

Tiger sharks are distributed throughout the world in tropical and warm-temperate seas, including off the east and west coasts of the United States, where they range in the Atlantic from Cape Cod to Florida and the Gulf of Mexico, and in the Pacific from southern California southward; they are as much at home in the shallows as they are in deep waters; and although it would be an exaggeration to say they are always hungry, they are recognized as particularly voracious hunters, not fussy about what they eat. The little one that bit Manolo, for instance, had swallowed a number of fish, a smaller member of its own kind, a cork net float, a rusty can, a grapefruit-sized wad of cotton waste and a table-tennis ball. In fact, there does not appear to be anything that a hunting tiger shark will not try to swallow. And when a tiger's stomach becomes full of indigestible junk, it will regurgitate and get rid of it. When not stimulated by hunger, however, the tiger is generally slow moving and seemingly docile; but, as Manolo discovered, it is fast, agile and tenaciously aggressive when attacked or disturbed.

Adult tiger sharks generally attain a length of between 11 and 14 feet and weigh 900 to 1,500 pounds, but exceptional individuals may exceed 18 feet in length and weigh more than 2,000 pounds, making this fish one of the most formidable to be encountered in the ocean. It is also one of the easiest to identify, for it offers many recognizable characteristics.

Seen underwater and from the side, the straight back of the adults, the relatively short, blunt nose, the long, pointed tail fin and a protuberant stomach can be noted from a distance, even before an observer can distinguish the characteristic vertical bars that mark their dorsal surfaces and from which the species derives its common name. Juveniles differ in that the head and nose are somewhat downturned, marring the straight-line effect; and the bars have not yet formed, showing instead as a series of mottled, irregularly shaped black patches. In those parts of the body not marked by either bars or patches, color is variable; the upper parts may be bluish gray, greenish gray or almost as black as the bars, while the undersides may be light gray, off-yellow or white.

Although the majority of species belonging to the Carcharhinidae family are viviparous, a few, including the tiger shark, are ovoviviparous: the embryos, each in its own egg, hatch about one year after fertilization. Somewhat like the blue shark, which belongs to the same family, tiger females produce large litters: as many as 50 pups have been counted, the newborns measuring between 26 and 34 inches in length.

Reference to the International Shark Attack File (SAF) shows that the number of people attacked by tiger sharks is exceeded only by the number of individuals struck by white sharks. But before recounting some of the documented attacks, it will help to keep matters in perspective if the SAF itself is briefly examined.

In 1958, Dr. Sydney Galler of the United States Office of Naval Research gathered together 34 scientists from four continents in order to examine the possibility of finding a more effective shark repellent. The meeting took place in New Orleans, Louisiana; it led to the formation of a shark research panel. Soon afterward, the panel became affiliated with the Hydrobiology Committee of the American Institute of Biological Sciences. Dr. Perry Gilbert, a veteran shark researcher, was asked to compile an international shark attack file. Later, Dr. Leonard Schultz of the Smithsonian Institution was given charge of the file, and for the next nine years, he and others investigated every shark attack report that they could uncover, meanwhile gathering volumes of information. Painstakingly, the team sifted through the mass of reports that came in from around the world, investigating every case as thoroughly as possible and recording only those cases that were backed by reasonably reliable evidence. In 1973, a total of 1,652 cases of shark attacks against humans had been recorded, the earliest of which took place in the year 1580 somewhere between Portugal and India when a seaman fell overboard a sailing ship (SAF Case 462). The ship's log recorded that "a large monster called *tiburon*...tore him to pieces before our very eyes. That surely was a grievous death."

The total number of cases recorded by the SAF up to 1973 included 168 strikes made against boats and 105 instances where sharks attacked an unknown number of victims of sea disasters. The work has continued since then, and the total has risen by an average of about 28 attacks per year worldwide.

Dr. H. David Baldridge, who has worked on developing shark repellent, was heavily involved in the production of the SAF, the history of which he has recorded in his book *Shark Attack*. In this work, Dr. Baldridge examines some of the factors that may have influenced a number of the attacks and he includes 200 case histories that detail some of the events that appear to have led the sharks to attack their victims. Naturally, all attacks became public knowledge immediately after each occurrence, but the value of *Shark Attack* and the SAF lies in the fact that all the incidents have been brought together reliably and make available a factual, accurate record.

After studying the SAF, courtesy of the Smithsonian Institution, and cross-checking its information with my own data and that gathered by other researchers, I have concluded that it is almost impossible to determine which species of shark poses the greatest threat to swimmers, divers or victims of sea disasters despite evidence that the great white and tiger sharks have attacked more people than any other species of selachian.

It is my view that all sharks are potentially dangerous, and it follows that the bigger the shark, the better it is able to kill a human. It is misleading to seek to determine which species is most dangerous, for I know that a swimmer or diver may be ignored by a white or tiger, yet come under attack from some smaller and seemingly less aggressive species.

It is reasonable and useful to count, as the SAF has done, the number of people attacked by a particular species of shark and to deduce from this total which kind of selachian has been guilty of the most strikes; but as will be noted in this chapter, the identity of the sharks responsible for the overwhelming majority of attacks has not been determined. In view of this, the prudent person will leave the water the moment he becomes aware of the presence of any kind of shark.

Out of 1,652 documented attacks compiled up to 1973, the identity of the sharks responsible for 1,385 strikes (83.84 percent of the total) has never been established. Of the remaining 267 cases (16.16 percent), it was not always possible to obtain positive identification, although there was apparently enough circumstantial evidence with which to indict particular species. Bearing these things in mind, the SAF shows that great whites were responsible for 32 of the 267 attacks, tigers struck a further 27 people and makos attacked 18. In the remaining 190 cases, 53 different species of sharks were thought to be accountable for one or more attacks. These SAF statistics clearly suggest that anyone who enters the world of the sharks should do so with caution. Indeed, it has been my contention that every individual who enters waters in which sharks are known to congregate should learn as much as possible about the habits of these powerful predators.

THERE ARE ABOUT three dozen species of sharks that are known to attack humans; but in view of the fact that the majority of strikes against humans have been committed by unidentified selachians, there can be little comfort in knowing that only 10.3 percent of some 350 different species would make it a practice to attack people. The fact is that, of the remaining 89.7 percent, the majority are capable of inflicting some form of injury if given cause to attack swimmers or divers, as the following case reports will show.

In 1972, while doing research in the North Pacific Ocean in Queen Charlotte Strait, I had just completed a dive in coastal waters during which I had been fascinated by the presence of a large school of dogsharks, or dogfish, as they are variously called. These sharks, members of the Squalidae family, are common bottom feeders found throughout the world, and they are represented by some 75 different species, 25 of which occur in North America. Ranging from seven-inch midgets (*Etmopterus bullisi*) to thirteen-foot giants (*Echinorhinus cookei*, or prickly shark), none are deemed to be dangerous to man. The species I had observed were Pacific dogfish (*Squalua suckleyi*), which grow to about five feet in length.

My boat, *The Stella Maris*, was anchored in a sheltered cove a short distance from Port Hardy, a community located on the northeast coast of Vancouver Island, British Columbia. Soon after I had left the chill water in order to change into warm clothing, a small open boat came in, a lone man sitting at the controls of the outboard motor. He waved as he passed, steered for the nearby shore and cut his motor, securing the boat to a natural "dock" of flat rock. Thereafter, he dragged a respectable catch of salmon out of his boat, found a comfortable place beside the water and began to clean his catch, throwing the heads and intestines into the water.

We chatted as he worked, and I told him about the large number of dogsharks I had seen on the bottom, almost directly below the place where he was sitting. He greeted this with a curse, explaining that he had been trying to catch some red snappers that very morning but had given up because his baits were invariably taken by the dogfish.

"I caught nine of the darned things!" he complained, explaining that he had killed them and thrown them back into the sea.

Soon after this conversation, the man cleaned his last fish, then leaned toward the water and started to rinse his hands. My back was turned, so I didn't see the entire action, but then I heard the fisherman's anguished yell. He was flailing at the water with his left hand while a large dogfish clung to the small finger of his right. Seconds later the shark dropped into the water and blood spurted from the injured digit. I was moving toward my dinghy when the man yelled, "Help me! It's taken the joint off my damned finger!"

Paddling furiously toward shore, I remember thinking that the fisherman was exaggerating; but when I reached him, I saw that the last joint of his little finger had been amputated as cleanly as though by surgery! Since I had come without my first-aid box, I removed one of the laces from my running shoes and used it as a tourniquet to stop the spurting blood. I rowed him back to *The Stella*, disinfected the wound and dressed it, after which I made tea with lots of sugar and wrapped a blanket around him, for he was in shock. While he sat shaking in the cabin, I weighed anchor and took him to Port Hardy, where he was treated at the small local clinic.

This attack was invited; it may be the first on record by a Pacific dogfish. The shark, which I judged to be about four feet long, had obviously been feeding on the offal that the fisherman was throwing in the water. When the man thrust his hands into the sea, the gore on them had caused the shark to strike.

On the other side of the Pacific 11 years earlier, an Australian fisherman was bitten in the throat by a small shark (SAF Case 869) that, although taken out of the water, refused to let go. Even after the shark's head had been severed from the body, the jaws held their viselike grip until they were surgically removed. Although two different accounts of this incident had been recorded, it appears that this, too, was an invited attack, occurring after the man had jokingly lifted the shark near his face. SAF records show that two other attacks by different species of dogfish have occurred.

The tendency of some sharks to clamp their jaws tightly on a victim is not unusual, although it is more common with small sharks. SAF Case 707 reports that in 1958, in the Canal Zone of Panama, a boy was taken to hospital with a small dead shark fixed tightly to one arm. Case 1284 refers to a Florida spearfisherman who, near Miami in 1963, found a four-foot nurse shark hiding within a rocky overhang. The man sought to drag the shark out by the tail, whereupon it turned and clamped its jaws on his left arm. A companion tried to remove the shark by stabbing it in the head several times, but the nurse shark hung on. Eventually, the victim managed to free his arm and was fortunate to get away with only minor lacerations.

Carelessness and downright foolhardy behavior will cause normally inoffensive sharks to fight back, a natural reaction that serves to show that all sharks are capable of injuring humans. The bigger the shark, the more serious the injuries and the more difficult it becomes to determine the motives underlying the attack.

Here again are some examples taken from the International Shark Attack File. All the selachians involved were large; the injuries inflicted were serious and in some cases fatal.

Case 1247 documents a great white shark's attack on a scuba diver in the waters off the Farallon Islands in California, in January 1964. The 21-year-old man was spearfishing in about 40 feet of water and had just impaled a rockfish when he ran short of air and had to make for the surface. Up to this point, neither the man nor other divers in the vicinity were aware that a large shark was nearby, despite the fact that the attacker was later estimated to measure between 20 and 25 feet and would have weighed more than 3,000 pounds!

As the victim reached the surface, the great white shark struck. It clamped its jaws on the man's legs from a point at midcalf to high up the thighs. Yet the diver reported later that he felt no pain and it was not until he actually saw the huge shark that he realized what had happened.

A number of other survivors of attacks by large sharks have reported that during the first moments of a strike they neither felt pain nor realized they had been attacked. My theory of this is based upon four specific factors: first, individuals attacked suddenly by a shark of whose presence they are unaware and which does not draw attention to itself by engaging in the more usual preambles preceding an attack (i.e., rub-bumping against the victim or butting violently with its snout) are relaxed and therefore not *anticipating* pain; second, the pressure exerted by the jaws of a large shark is enormous (in excess of three tons per square inch of surface), and this dampens the sensitivity of the pain-conducting nerves; third, the teeth of sharks are nearly razorblade-sharp and cut quickly and cleanly; and fourth, because of heat loss in water below 68°F, human tissue is less sensitive to pain.

It is significant to note that in the SAF case just quoted, the air temperature was 64°F and the water temperature was 55°F. During immersion studies carried out by U.S. naval researchers, it was discovered that at 68°F, the body temperature of a swimmer levels off after about one hour's exposure, and in water above that temperature, heat production in humans appears to keep pace with heat loss. Other studies show that below 68°F, body temperature continues to drop; at 60°F, a swimmer runs a 50 percent risk of losing consciousness after two hours of exposure unless protected by special apparel. It follows, of course, that below 60°F, body temperature drops rapidly; and even though Case 1247 was wearing a full wetsuit, his temperature would have dropped below normal by the time he was forced to surface when the air in his tanks had become exhausted.

When this victim realized he was gripped by the jaws of a shark, he slammed the point of his speargun against the white's snout, whereupon it let go and the diver was helped to safety by a companion. Meanwhile, five other divers on the bottom, evidently unaware of what had been going on, were threatened by the enormous shark. It forced two of them to seek shelter in a cave, then threatened the other three. In this way, going for one group of divers or another, it kept them from surfacing for about five minutes, then, as suddenly as it had arrived, it left.

The attack victim recovered. He had suffered multiple cuts on both legs, a deep gash on the back of one thigh, which exposed the bone, and another deep cut on the back of one calf, which severed a main nerve, a wound that impaired the use of the foot. During surgery, a fragment of tooth was recovered from the thigh wound; it proved to belong to a large white shark.

Two years earlier, in 1962, Case 1001, another spearfisherman was attacked in water off the Farallon Islands. As in Case 1247, the attack took place in January and water temperature was below 60°. After chasing a fish — again, at a depth of 40 feet — the diver rose to the surface and was immediately attacked.

" It hit me just as I surfaced. At first I thought it was a seal, but a seal doesn't have a mouth that big! It hit me first from the right side and started shaking me like a dog plays with a bone. I spit out my mouthpiece and began yelling: 'Shark! Shark!' At the same time I jabbed at the shark's snout with my spear. He let loose of me and took off," the victim reported.

During the time that the injured man was being helped to safety and other divers were warned to get out of the water, the shark, estimated to be between 14 and 15 feet long but not definitely identified as a great white, remained in the neighborhood and was seen following a diver who was unaware of its presence. The victim, flown by helicopter to hospital, was treated for deep leg wounds and a severe gash in one buttock.

What may well be the most horrifying shark attack ever recorded took place in the waters off New Jersey in 1916, when four people were killed and one injured in the space of ten days by what may well have been one particular shark, a great white that measured eight feet six inches.

The first attack took place off Beach Haven on July 2, when a 24-year-old man was swimming toward the beach and was about 100 yards from shore. People on the beach first saw a shark fin appear on the surface behind the bather (Case 202) and then watched in horror as the shark struck. An unidentified man courageously swam to the victim and helped him ashore, seemingly driving the shark away by his arrival. The victim's legs had been severely lacerated and he died from loss of blood and shock before reaching hospital.

The next attack took place July 6 at Spring Lake, higher up the New Jersey coast. A 28-year-old man was swimming some distance from shore when spectators saw him disappear suddenly and noted blood staining the surface of the water (Case 399). Lifeguards went to the rescue by boat. When they reached the victim, he gasped: "Shark got me! Bit off my legs!" Shortly afterward, he died. The right leg was bitten off halfway below the knee; the left foot and part of the ankle were also gone, and most of the leg had been almost completely stripped of flesh. The shark had also removed a section on the right side of the abdomen.

On the afternoon of July 12, the shark struck again, this time in Matawan Creek, near the community of the same name, and some 25 miles from where the last victim had been attacked. The creek is only about 35 feet wide and runs for some 15 miles to empty in Raritan Bay. It is reported that some hours before the attack, two men saw the large, dark outline of a fish swimming up creek, but when a group of boys bathing in the creek were told about this sighting, they disregarded the warning, undoubtedly thinking that no shark would be encountered so far from the sea.

One of the boys, a 12-year-old, was floating on his back watched by a companion who was standing thigh-deep in the water. The friend felt something brush hard against his legs and reportedly saw the tail of a large fish moments before the floating youngster was struck and dragged down into the murky water (Case 204). A courageous young man went into the water to try and rescue the boy. He too was attacked, his right leg stripped of flesh from groin to right knee (Case 205). He died in hospital.

Later that same day, another boy (Case 206) was attacked. He and some companions had been swimming about half a mile downstream of the place where the other two victims had been struck. This youngster recovered, but it is not clear from conflicting testimony whether or not he lost one leg.

Following these attacks, an undetermined number of sharks were caught in Matawan Creek and in Raritan Bay. One of these, the eight-and-a-half-foot white shark mentioned, had 15 pounds of human flesh and bones in its stomach, including a boy's anklebone and a section of human rib.

The white shark (*Carcharodon carcharias*) is the most powerful member of the Lamnidae, or mackerel shark, family. And it is certainly the largest. The record to date stands at 21 feet for a shark taken off the Cuban coast in 1940. It weighed 4,800 pounds! More recently, it is claimed that a white measuring slightly more than 29 feet was taken in the Atlantic, near the Portuguese Azores Islands. If the existence of such a monster is confirmed by experts, it will strengthen the view — held by a minority of scientists — that the white's gigantic ancestor, *Carcharodon megalodon*, is still alive, although it is more generally thought to have become extinct some 50,000 years ago. This creature is believed to have measured between 50 and 80 feet in length, a deduction based upon fossil teeth.

The fact that the known record stands at 21 feet does not deny the probability that white sharks considerably larger than that are to be found in the oceanic deeps. Even the most cautious scientists admit that whites up to 26 feet long are likely to exist, while sightings made by reliable observers strengthen the opinion that enormous whites — or perhaps their ancient relatives — are abroad in our seas.

Tiger sharks, conversely, are numerous and found worldwide in tropical and warm-temperate waters. And these sharks, second only to the white in the number of victims they are known to have attacked, seem inclined to bite off more than they can chew, for even small ones will strike at adult humans.

Large tigers, naturally, do the most damage. One that was estimated at 20 feet swallowed an adult diver in June 1949 (Case 376). The victim and a companion were searching for abalone in about 30 feet of water in the area of La Jolla, California. The victim's companion had just surfaced when his friend was thrust out of the water about 60 feet from the witness. The victim screamed and called for help, then disappeared under the surface. His companion, believing the diver had suffered a severe cramp, dove under, searching. Then he saw his friend from a distance of about five feet, that is to say, he saw his head and shoulders protruding out of the mouth of an enormous shark that lay on the bottom and would not give up the victim, who was evidently already dead. The body was never recovered.

Another tiger shark attacked and killed a 12-year-old boy in the waters off Lanikai, on the island of Oahu, Hawaii, in December 1958 (Case 405). The attacker, seen later from a search boat, amputated the victim's right leg from the knee downward. The body was not recovered until later, but since no other serious injuries were found, it is practically certain that the shark made only one strike. Whether the attacker was 15 feet long or 25 has never been determined, but there is no doubt that the shark was large, for those searching for the boy's body reported that the fish continued to cruise the sea, swimming on the surface, its protruding dorsal fin measuring about 18 inches in height.

These accounts of shark attacks are recorded here to show that all sharks are dangerous in certain situations. The few cases quoted here took place before 1973. There have been more recent attacks, but when one considers the hundreds of thousands of bathers who crowd the world's beaches and coastal waters each summer, an individual's chances of becoming a victim are smaller than that of being struck by lightning.

Sharks continue to fascinate me. They are such *efficient* beings, so gorgeous when observed in their own world and so well adjusted to their environment. Compared to the large land carnivores, there is no doubt that selachians are less guilty of injuring or killing humans. The lion, for instance, which has been eulogized since Biblical times and is looked upon as the "king of beasts," has killed far more people than the shark; so has the tiger. But both of these powerful hunters have always received "good press." We see them as regal beasts, and we admire their strength and their beauty, realizing that they can be dangerous, but continuing to think of them as mammals worthy of our respect. No sane tourist, of course, would stroll about carelessly among lions or tigers, yet tourists disport themselves almost naked in the domain of the sharks and are frequently guilty of actually inviting attack.

In the many years that I have been studying the natural world, I have come to respect all wild beings and to see them in their true perspective, organisms that have each been created for a particular purpose and that, together, contribute to the well-being and continuity of the world's natural environments, sharks no less so than any other animals. Unfortunately, however, because selachians live in a habitat that poses enormous difficulties for those who wish to study it, the behavior of these interesting fish is still not well understood. As a result, the majority of people find it hard, if not impossible, to view them with sympathy and understanding.

As the sharks themselves have taught me, they much prefer to mind their own business provided they are not interfered with. The majority of them behave peacefully when not engaged in hunting for their natural food. They do not like trespassers, but even when they are encroached upon, they rarely attack without first warning of their intention to do so, giving an intruder an opportunity to retreat. If we ever manage to understand the rules governing territorial etiquette within the world of sharks, it may well be possible to greatly reduce the number of attacks.

As a child, I became fond of sharks I kept as pets, the majority accepting me as fully as I accepted them. They quickly learned to recognize me and to understand that whenever I entered the water I invariably carried food with me. Never once was I bitten. Later, as an adult, my views became altered by mythology and biological training to such an extent that, for some years, I lost my appreciation of sharks, thinking of them as *specimens* that could be killed or otherwise used for experiments in the "cause of science." It was not until I began to do research in Angola that I once again started to think of sharks as fellow beings.

THE GREAT WHITE IS THE LARGEST SHARK.
ONE SPECIMEN ATTAINED 36 FEET AND
WEIGHED ALMOST 2 TONS.

# Chapter 6

✿

THE TWENTY or so Angolan sharks of various sizes and species that had been competing for the food which one of my topside assistants was dropping into the water suddenly sheared away from the immediate vicinity of my makeshift anti-shark shelter. Remaining afterward in the area, but seen only as slowly gliding, shadowy forms, these selachians, which had been keeping me company for almost two weeks, lured by the gifts of food, had not behaved in such a manner before this. They surprised me on two counts: immediately before they moved off they had been feeding actively and competing vigorously for every scrap of fish that hit the surface, giving no indication that they had lost their appetite; then, too, when the moment of departure arrived, every shark in sight left almost at the same instant.

Something had obviously disturbed the sharks, but as I looked through each of my three portholes, I could not detect anything unusual in the submarine world. And the schools of small fish that were forever busy snapping up the crumbs left by their formidable relatives remained in the area, now attacking the food undisturbed. I had just about decided that the sharks had left because they *had* eaten enough when I saw the shadowy form moving toward my shelter. Too distant yet to distinguish its species, its shape and the way it moved identified it as a shark. A *big* one. Moments later I knew what kind it was, even though I still couldn't make out its color or even see it distinctly. This was the creature I had been hoping to see ever since I was told that at least one of its kind habitually patrolled the island from which my metal tube was suspended. The great white shark, Mr. Big himself, a lazily swimming, arrogant, supremely powerful animal that moves like no other selachian.

Fascinated yet unable to conquer fear, I watched the white as it approached. At first, it seemed as though it was going to pass in front of me; then, just as I could make out its white underbelly and gray-black upper body, it angled toward me. I estimated it measured about 16 feet, but as it neared my shelter, coming head on with its great mouth slightly open and revealing ragged bottom teeth, what impressed me most was its enormous girth. With stiff pectoral fins pointing downward, large black eyes, nostrils like twin, horizontal commas, and heavy snout, the white seemed more than three feet wide and just about as deep. Then it approached at a three-quarter, head-on angle. The creature's right eye was not visible, but its hypnotic, anthracite-black left orb was fixed on my face.

How does one describe such a stare? The eye was by no means expressionless, yet it showed neither aggression nor neutrality. The glow of life that it contained was perhaps triggered by a need to appraise the strange object that swayed against the rock face. There was keen intelligence in that eye, although it was not remotely like the eyes of any mammal I had ever seen. To me, at that moment and to this day, the impression was that I was being appraised by an alien intelligence, by a being in control of itself and its environment, by a being that knew not the meaning of fear or any other emotions in my own kind as well as in the hundreds of land animals with which I had become close.

My fear reached its crescendo when the behemoth's unwinking eye came within 18 inches of my face. At that instant I was sure the white was going to bump into my shelter, and although I had previously been confident of the strength of the iron and of the stranded wire cable that suspended it from the surface, I was close to panic when I thought about what this great shark could do to my air hose and the hemp lifeline that was my only link to the surface. I was wearing an old-fashioned hard-hat diving outfit, complete with heavy rubber suit, brass helmet and lead-soled boots. In this outfit, my chances of ever reaching my own world alive would be nil if the white attacked and got tangled in my crucial lines. Then, with a mere flick of its great, moon-shaped tail, the big fish altered course away from the shelter and the rock cliff, its enormous pectoral actually hitting the tube with its tip, rocking me and making a soft grating sound as it touched.

Maintaining an easy movement, the white steered toward open water but appeared to be angling upward. As its tail passed within three or four feet of my center porthole, I was able to see its claspers and determine that it was a male. Soon, the great fish became an amorphous shadow. Moments later, the outline of the big body became a blur, but now I was sure it was heading toward the surface. As it disappeared, I felt four tugs on my signal line, a prearranged code that told of the presence of a large shark on the surface. I acknowledged with one pull before settling down to observe the sea around me.

The smaller sharks that had given the white plenty of sea room began returning, led by two good-sized shortfin makos, one about nine feet long, the other perhaps ten feet. Some distance to the left of these fat fish were three narrow-toothed sharks (*Carcharhinus brachyurus*), each about the same size at between five and six feet. Distinguished by a deep body, fairly long and pointed nose, a brownish back and sides, and light underparts, the common name of this species is derived from the shape of its teeth, which are sharply pointed, narrow and somewhat triangular, with extremely fine serrated edges. These sharks are reported to attack humans, but since I had been exposed to them twice daily now for 12 days and had noted that, though they followed my descents and ascents, they never came closer than about 20 feet, I considered them to be docile. This is more than I can say for the feisty black-tips, which were always present and in good supply. Invariably, these little sharks, about four feet on average, exhibited a lot of interest in me each time I went down and returned to the surface, although they never actually tried to attack.

Undoubtedly because of the fish that my surface crew kept dropping in my vicinity, I always had lots of company, although the species changed from time to time and day to day. Apart from a variety of conventional fish, some of which I could identify and many which were new to me, the ubiquitous dogsharks were always present, at times in large numbers of up to 30 or so, on other occasions represented by two or three of their kind. On several occasions, tiger sharks had nosed in, one of which I estimated to be eight feet long, the rest small, mostly under five feet.

The bigger sharks usually stayed a relatively short time, perhaps an hour or two, but the smaller fry were almost permanent visitors, remaining nearby even when food was not being dropped into the water. Now, however, as though to make up for the time they had lost when the white arrived, the entire crew became exceptionally active. I signalled topside, two long pulls followed by two short ones, to tell my helpers to stop throwing dead fish into the water, for I needed to go to the surface and I was afraid that the darting, excitable crew outside my shelter might soon go into a feeding frenzy. Moments later, I changed my mind about leaving my shelter!

As before, the lesser sharks cleared off. The white appeared 2 minutes and 23 seconds later, this time coming in from the left and remaining a good 15 feet away from me. Despite the murky water, I knew that the big fish was again giving me that impassive stare. I signalled topside, this time giving three short tugs on the rope, which meant I wanted more fish dropped into the water. When the first two fish hit, then slowly started to sink, the white turned, nosed upward, opened its giant mouth and sucked the food in without visible effort. In this way, the white ingested eight fish, none of which was longer than 18 inches.

Watching the performance, it struck me as ludicrous that such a monster fish should even bother to take snacks. He reminded me of an obese person absentmindedly munching on an occasional olive! In any event, after he had eaten those eight sea basses, I signalled above to put a stop to any more feeding, for I was getting cold and did not want to come out of my shelter and be hauled up while Mr. Big was sailing in my waters. I was now anxious for my large neighbor to leave, for my hands and feet were getting numb from the cold.

THE EVENTS that were to lead to my encounter with a great white shark were set in train in May 1963 when I left Canada on a journey that was to take me to Portugal, the Azores Islands, Portuguese Guinea, Cape Verde Islands, the Congo, Angola and Mozambique — a dual expedition during which I was to investigate the political affairs of Portugal's African colonies for journalistic purposes while taking the opportunity to do some shark research.

During the last half of May and throughout June, I had gone on a number of shark-fishing trips in the Atlantic, starting in the area of the Azores, then off the Guinea coast and lastly in the waters around the Cape Verde Islands. In July, I was land-bound for two weeks in the Congo, after which I went south to Angola. On July 26, I settled down for a spell in Luanda, the capital city located on the coast about eight degrees south of the equator. Here, I began to make plans to do some diving. At first, I intended to rent scuba equipment but decided instead to hire a hard-hat outfit, believing this would allow me to remain under-water longer and keep me stationary in an antishark cage. I hoped to blend into the submarine environment and be looked upon as a neutral, *inedible* organism.

A few inquiries soon led me to Joaquim Gomes, a man in his early forties and about my own size. Joaquim earned his living as a diver, engaging in salvage operations and doing repair work underwater when needed. He readily agreed to rent me his equipment, and we eventually struck a deal that included the hiring of Joaquim as well as his two assis-tants, Agostinho Rodriges and Manoel Teixeira, the former about thirty years old, the latter a stocky youth in his early twenties with shoulders so wide as to make him look deformed, a barrel chest, and arms that seemed almost as thick as my legs! As his build suggested, Manoel was enormously strong, a happy-go-lucky young bull of a man who turned out to be a great asset to my venture.

My newly acquired assistants were of mixed parentage, the result of unions between Portuguese and Bacongo Africans.

Sitting in the bar of Luanda's main hotel with Joaquim, Agostinho and Manoel, each of us sipping a glass of wine as a toast to our new relationship, I felt at ease at the prospect of entrusting my life to these three men. Each of them gave me a strong and immediate feeling of confidence. They were practical men, unquestionably honest, experienced in the ways of the sea, and they had all risked their lives at one time or another in pursuit of a dangerous living. Joaquim had twice been attacked by small sharks, and he carried the scars of their teeth on his left arm and right calf. The last encounter had occurred two years earlier as he was being raised from the bottom and was only about 15 feet from the surface.

Relating the experience to me in Portuguese — which I speak reasonably well — Joaquim pointed to Manoel, smiled and explained further: "And this idiot here . . . what does he do? He's in the boat and he sees what's happening, so he dives in the water holding an iron bar. Then he poked the shark in the gills. It ran away! He's a fool this one! But a good boy, eh?" Manoel made a rude hand gesture toward his employer and turned to smile at me, shrugging his massive shoulders before returning to toy with his glass of red wine.

That same afternoon, we all gathered in Joaquim's small, dockside workshop-cum-storeroom, where I was introduced to the equipment that was to be placed at my disposal. Since I had never used hard-hat equipment, Joaquim gave me some preliminary instruction, during which I dressed in his suit, helmet and lead-soled boots. The rubber suit fit me quite well, although the boots were somewhat large.

Afterward, we left the building to inspect Joaquim's bargelike boat, a clinker-built wooden hull powered by diesel. It had an open top and a decked bottom, and it was 26 feet long with a beam of 13 feet at midships with a rounded stern and a blunt, tuglike bow. The outside of the hull was sheathed in copper to prevent fouling by barnacles and tunneling by shipworm, a misnamed little animal that is not a worm but a clam of the genus *Teredo*. It has modified its shell, turning it into a drill with which to tunnel into the wood of boats, dock pilings and driftwood logs. This destructive task is further aggravated by the efforts of another wood-borer, the gribble, a minute crustacean of the genus *Limnoria* that resembles a white pill bug, or wood louse. Although only about one-eighth of an inch long, this midget with 14 legs can do great damage to a ship's timbers by force of numbers; several hundred of them often being found per square inch of wood.

Being a tyro in the use of Joaquim's equipment, I inspected everything with great care, paying particular attention to the diving gear, air line and the ropes and cables that were to be used to lower and raise me in the water. Later Joaquim had Agostinho start the diesel motor that powered the air pump, showing me how this worked and how the air entered the helmet and my breath exited through a pressure valve. When this was done, the diver showed me a second motor and pump, spares in the event of failure in the main air system. This auxiliary was also started and tested.

Similar to Pedro Roquena's gear, all of Joaquim's equipment was old yet in perfect shape, a characteristic shared by all professional sailors and marine workers, whose lives depend on careful maintenance. Because of the vagaries of their trades, they can rarely afford the luxury of owning brand-new gear.

Joaquim suggested I go out with him and his crew the next morning to try out the diving suit in relatively shallow water just outside the harbor, explaining that he wanted me to have confidence in his gear while at the same time he needed to feel confident in my ability to use it. Apart from testing my behavior underwater and working out the rope-tug codes so essential to communication when the diver has no radio links with the surface, Joaquim needed to make sure that I was not one of those people who suffer from claustrophobia and are thus likely to panic when below the surface with a great brass helmet bolted in place. Thinking about this as the diver talked, I too wondered if I might react negatively to the experience. Earlier, although the helmet had only been tried to check the fit and had not been bolted in place, I had experienced a slight sense of confinement.

As matters turned out, I did feel a sense of claustrophobia as soon as Manoel began tightening the bolts; this got worse when I tried to move and needed to be assisted by Agostinho and Joaquim — each of my feet seemed to be encased in cement and my neck muscles pulled against the weight of the awkward, heavy headpiece. For some seconds I was on the point of cancelling out, but, controlling my fear, I reached the stern ladder, got on the first rung and slowly lowered myself below the surface. Immediately I became immersed, I attained negative buoyancy, and as I found myself again looking at the submarine world, my apprehension vanished.

I went down 40 feet to the bottom, paved by fine, white sand, some boulders and patches of kelp, their slowly waving fronds reaching above my head. Walking was not hard, but my rate of progress was snaillike, and I got the feeling I was watching my environment projected onto a cine screen in slow motion. I was restricted by the twin lines that connected me to the surface, and for this reason, the extraordinary sense of freedom one feels when using scuba equipment was completely lacking. In fact, because only my bare hands were in contact with the sea, I had the impression I was looking under the water from a glass-bottomed boat, rather than being submerged.

Preoccupied with these impressions, I didn't realize for some minutes that visibility was good, for the strong African sun bathed the bottom in soft yellowish light; only in those areas where the tall kelp plants were profuse did deep shadows form. And it was there that I saw my first Angolan sharks — small, sluggish sandbar sharks (*Carcharhinus plumbeus*), none of which were much longer than two feet. This species is cosmopolitan in distribution; it is said to grow to a maximum length of eight feet and rarely rises to the surface.

Mingling with the young sandbars were a number of dogfish, most of which were about three feet long. At my approach, all the sharks scuttled into the shelter of the kelp beds, leaving as my only companions a number of small, conventional fish, some of which came over to inspect my shiny helmet.

Interested as I was in my environment, time passed quickly, and I was startled when Joaquim gave the signal to return to the surface by tugging my tether line twice, which meant I had been down for half an hour. I began to work my way back toward the boat, the hull of which showed some distance away as a black, bobbing shadow. As I walked, I did not feel the least bit chilled. This, however, was not surprising, for the air temperature was 106°F, and the water temperature at the surface had registered 78°F. At the forty-foot level, my wrist thermometer showed a temperature of 71°F. It was almost like taking a warm bath!

Joaquim, who was to supervise all my dives, brought me back to the surface much more slowly than I would have thought necessary for decompression from such shallow dives; but as he explained later, he always played it safe, taking longer to rise than was strictly necessary. In this way, he avoided the risk of nitrogen narcosis, or caisson disease, otherwise known as the bends, which develops when rising from an atmosphere of high pressure to air of normal pressure. The condition is caused when bubbles of nitrogen are released into the blood during a too rapid change of pressure. Even a mild case of the bends is *nasty*, so I was not at all sorry that Joaquim tended to err on the side of caution!

My test dive had convinced me that Joaquim was reliable and more than capable of fulfilling his part of our deal. He was equally convinced that I could handle my end of it. We then discussed the area in which I was to conduct my research and the way in which I was going to do it.

I wanted to become accepted as a part of the undersea world. I wanted to be protected from shark attack during the time I was submerged. I wanted to find a location far enough from the port of Luanda that would offer the following characteristics: the depth should be no greater than 300 feet, preferably somewhat less; there should be at least one rock face that would protect my back if need arose; the water should be as clear as possible; boat traffic should be minimal; suitable anchorage, or docking, should be available for the diving boat; and, most important, sharks should be known to dwell in the area.

As I listed these requirements, Joaquim kept nodding. When I finished, he smiled, reached for a marine chart and pointed out a small island that was located to the south of Luanda and, so he said, about an hour's run away. Here, on the west side of the island, the rock dropped sheer, offering an ideal backing for whatever antishark cage I might eventually use. The depth, according to the chart, was 98.42 feet near the base of the submarine cliff, increasing accordingly as the bottom shelved.

In this area, Joaquim said, I would encounter many sharks, especially if we chummed the waters with fish. Also, it was known that one or more great white sharks visited the seaward side of the island on a fairly regular basis.

Since this location suited my needs admirably, we next discussed the possibility of renting an antishark cage. This was a short debate. There was no such thing available in Angola. Joaquim was positive about this because he had been trying to locate one for some time. Nevertheless, he had *made* one of his own design, but had not yet used it. Would I see it?

The thing was simple. It consisted of an eight-foot corrugated-steel culvert that had a diameter of 39.37 inches. Welded to the bottom was a heavy, steel-mesh grill with two- by three-inch openings. The top consisted of a "lid" made out of the same mesh, but hinged so that it would open and with a space on one edge large enough to admit the air line and hoist rope. One round, 14-inch porthole had been cut into the culvert, its center coinciding with face height if a man crouched slightly; it was also mesh-covered. To complete the "cage," large U-bolts had been welded at the top, one on each side, with a heavy chain shackled to each side. This was for attaching the hoisting cable.

This homemade tubular shelter was more than adequate, except that I asked Joaquim if he could cut two more portholes, one to the left and the other to the right of the central opening. Also, since I thought it would be awkward for me to spend any length of time in a semistoop in order to watch the sea, I asked the diver if he could attach a small seat to what was to be the back of the tube, this to be hinged so that it could be swung out of the way during entry or exit and at the proper height so that, squatting on it, I could look out of any one of the three ports without strain. Joaquim thought that these improvements could easily be done by Agostinho, who immediately set about the task, promising that he would be finished by the next afternoon.

TWO DAYS AFTER Agostinho completed the work on the tube, we pulled away from the dock, Joaquim steering without benefit of compass but with an intimate knowledge of the coastline and its waters. The sky was cloudless, the heat stifling, even with the small breeze that was coming off the water; but dressed only in a pair of swim trunks, I managed to keep somewhat comfortable as I watched Luanda fall astern while admiring the blaze of color furnished by flowers that decorated practically every house balcony in the city. Even after we were too far away to notice detail, the riot of color persisted, resembling an enormous, impressionist mural in which reds and pinks predominated, their mass glowing fluorescently.

The big tube, now fitted with the extra ports and the small seat, lay forward, rocking from side to side with the movements of the barge. It was secured to the boat's hoist by hook and cable, by means of which it had been brought on board and would later be lowered into the water.

An hour after leaving the harbor, Luanda disappeared from view and the island which was our destination was visible to the southwest. At this time, the view was of the eastern face and the lush tree and shrub growth was becoming noticeable. Using field glasses, I saw a long, curved beach that was picturesquely backed by tropical vegetation. Not a person could be seen on the entire expanse of smooth, yellow sand, despite the fact that Joaquim had told me that a number of native African families lived on the islet. Although my thoughts immediately turned to swimming and beach lounging, I did not find it surprising that the paradisial crescent of sand was devoid of bathers, for few native Africans can swim, even those who earn their living by fishing. That inviting beach, I decided, was going to be my lodging place during those times when I was not engaged in research on the other side of the island.

My arrangements with Joaquim were that I would descend for two hours each morning and two hours each afternoon, except when the moon became full, in which case I would skip the afternoon descent and go down at night to experience the shark's world after dark. For night work, we agreed that the tube would be raised to within 20 feet of the surface for better visibility. My shelter could go up or down according to cloud conditions, but the normal position was at the 40-foot mark, suspended from shore and backed up against the rock face. Except for those times when I descended at night, Joaquim and his crew planned to return to Luanda during midmorning and each afternoon.

At first I had intended to journey with them, but the sight of the beach changed that. I would spend my leisure hours on the beach; and I would sleep there, under the stars, borrowing a tarpaulin from Joaquim in case of rain.

Discussing these things with Joaquim, he suggested it would be better if he dropped me off near the beach on his way home every day and Manoel could row me ashore in the dinghy. Otherwise, I would have at least an hour's walk morning and evening through some rough jungle country. Also, the diver said he would land with me that same day so as to talk with the local residents, explaining what I was doing on the island.

By the time these things had been settled, the barge had reached the far side of the isle; this presented an altogether different landscape from the landward coast. Flat rock paved the shoreline and climbed inland for about 200 feet. These circumstances offered ideal anchorage in deep water as well as a platform for the air pumps and engines and the rest of our equipment. Because of the rock's smooth face and its almost plumbline-straight descent, it was decided that the tube would remain in the water rather than being lowered and raised each day, for it would be an easy matter to alter its depth by raising or lowering it by hand because the weight of the contraption would be drastically reduced by the buoyancy of the sea. This meant, however, that I would have to travel up and down suspended by the lifeline, and thus unprotected during each journey; but since I wasn't going deep, I didn't think there was much risk involved. And if worse came to worst, the topside crew could always raise me and the tube to surface level, allowing me to leave the water in safety.

Having looked over the terrain, discussed strategy and lifted the anti-shark shelter out of the barge in readiness for its first descent, we paused for lunch. I told Joaquim I would not go down for four days, wanting the tube to remain unoccupied so as to allow the sharks and fish to become accustomed to it. Meanwhile, we would chum the water twice a day as of the next morning to encourage the sharks to visit the vicinity of the shelter. Joaquim would arrange with the island's fishermen residents to supply us with enough fish for our daily needs, an estimated 30 or 40 pounds. The chum would be dropped punctually at 11:00 a.m. and at 3:00 p.m. for the next four days; after that, when I was inside the shelter, Manoel would chum the water on my signal.

By three o'clock that afternoon, the tube was in place 40 feet down and all the gear was assembled, tested and ready to go. We now left the location, stopped over at the local village, where I met the residents and where fish supplies were agreed upon. I had no food supplies and wanted to collect some of my things from the hotel, as well as to ensure that my room was held for me, so I returned to Luanda with my three companions.

The next morning, just as Manoel was getting ready to go out in the dinghy to chum the water around my shelter with an assortment of fish of various species, I decided on impulse that I would first go down into the tube to test it — and to test myself! It would be preferable, I reasoned, to make my "maiden voyage" *before* the chum attracted the sharks, thereby accustoming myself to the descent and the rise without having to worry about inquisitive and hungry selachians.

Manoel stopped the outboard motor of the small boat, climbed ashore and he and Agostinho helped me into the diving suit while Joaquim started the auxiliary engine and tested the air line and helmet valves. Twenty minutes later, I was being assisted to the water's edge, where I sat down, heavy boots dangling out of sight, and then, with dry mouth and butterflies beating their wings inside my stomach, I slipped off the rock, dropping too swiftly at first but soon slowing as Manoel took hold of the lifeline. An instant later, I stopped moving altogether, but before I could determine the reason for the halt, the waters around me boiled up silently — I could hear nothing because of the row that was going on inside the helmet as air came in one valve and left out the other. The sudden upheaval scared the wits out of me, until Joaquim's face appeared before one of my little windows. He gestured, a thumbs-up movement of one hand, while he mouthed words. He was checking to make sure that everything was working well. I signalled back to him, giving the thumbs-up, then Joaquim returned to the surface.

Now I descended at a moderate rate. The water was almost warm and visibility was excellent, the powerful equatorial sun penetrating deeply into the sea. Before I realized it, my boots scraped against the top of the tube. I signalled to slow my descent, kicked away from the tube, reached forward clumsily and lifted the mesh lid. Pulling myself upward by clutching the lifeline with both hands, I positioned myself above the entrance and lowered myself inside, closing the lid and making sure that air hose and lifeline were nesting in their proper places. I signalled that I was now inside.

Despite my cumbersome equipment, I found that I had a reasonable amount of space in the tube, enough to allow me to turn and look through each porthole and to shift position. Also, by leaning backward, I could reach the meshed windows in order to put things into the water, which I intended to do during a series of experiments.

After satisfying myself on these counts, I flipped down the jump seat and looked out of the center porthole. I was startled to see a seven- or eight-foot shortfin mako moving about ten feet from my tube, almost level with my observation aperture!

Looking through the right port, I saw two more sharks, although these were too far away to identify. They were smaller than the mako, swimming in lazy arcs and keeping each other company, with only a few feet separating them.

Turning to the left window, I was further surprised to see five dogfish, all about the same length at some three feet from nose to tail. And cruising about without concern were a number of conventional fish, including some sea bass, caranxes and a few sea perches. Several dozen lesser fry were darting about, all eagerly mouthing the rock face. It was this behavior that suggested the reason for the presence of the sharks and fish: in lowering, the tube had repeatedly scraped against the rock, dislodging barnacles and other small life-forms. Its contact with the granite must have made considerable noise, producing scraping and booming sounds and creating pressure waves, no matter how small. These things must have brought my visitors. Undoubtedly they had been present even as I descended, but I had either been too busy to notice or the sharks had kept their distance. Watching the mako as it passed my shelter, I realized that nature had once again taught me not to prejudge the behavior of animals, no matter how sound my reasoning might be. I should, of course, have realized that the tube would cause pressure waves as it was being lowered; just as I ought to have been aware that its contact with the rock face would have the effect of dislodging hundreds of organisms and so expose them to the ever-waiting mouths of the fish. I should therefore have been expecting company and, although the sharks had made no threatening move, I ought to have been more alert during my descent. Above all else, I should have brought my shark stick.

As these thoughts were going through my mind, I continued to watch. The mako had gone about 30 yards away, completed a half circle and was now coming back my way. The other two sharks were also approaching and now I could identify them: tigers, the larger about six feet long, the other about five feet. Keeping clear of the mako, they swam in tandem but appeared to be far more interested in the rock face and the fish than in my tube or its occupant. Not so with the mako. It came up, moved to the left, turned and approached the tube, then circled away just before it struck the metal. Now it dived and I lost sight of it. The tigers continued swimming in front of me, but one darted upward and struck a careless sea bass that was probably about 14 inches long. In a trice, the fish disappeared inside the gullet of the shark, which continued its patrol in the same leisurely fashion.

For 20 minutes, I watched the two tigers as they moved in the vicinity of my shelter — their intention was to gulp down as many fish as they could catch. Seven times one or the other caught a fish; but rather than escape from the area, the other fish continued nuzzling and snapping at the rock face.

During this, my first descent, I wasn't ready to spend too long in the tube — I needed to get used to its confinement in stages — so I pulled the lifeline, signalling my wish to rise. Almost immediately, I felt the tug of the rope, and by the time I had opened the grilled trapdoor, I was already rising , having just enough time to close the circular gate before I was taken past it.

The test dive completed all the equipment checks, and since the tube was to remain unoccupied in the water for the next four days, I returned to Luanda with Joaquim and the others to collect my things and buy food, after which the barge was to return me to the island in the morning. It was decided that Manoel should stay with me so as to help chum the water in the area of the tube and to assist with other chores.

Early the next day, with a spare dinghy in tow — a wooden craft 12 feet long that Manoel and I would use to travel from the beach to the other side of the island — we left the harbor. By early afternoon of that same day, Manoel and I had erected a shelter out of canvas and posts, under which we could sleep in the event of rain, which could be torrential in that season. Afterward, we lounged on the beach until it was time to prepare fish for supper.

We had no means of preserving food, and I had only brought a few nonperishable items, such as a container of instant coffee and some cans of milk, seasoning, a small grill, two tin plates, a frying pan and two mugs. Flour, salt and baking powder to make bannock formed our only "luxury" food, besides the twice-daily supplies of fish that we bought from the local residents. For bedding, we each had two blankets, one to spread over the sand as a "mattress," and one as a cover.

The next three days passed quickly and pleasantly, each punctuated by an early morning swim and some island walking and socializing during those times when I wasn't helping Manoel chum the water. On several occasions, while we were throwing fish into the sea, small sharks rose to the surface. Once a large mako became busy eating every piece of fish that was thrown, and his presence kept the smaller selachians away.

At eleven o'clock on the morning of our fourth day on the island, I dressed for the dive, attended by Joaquim and Agostinho, and descended to the shelter, which was suspended at the 40-foot level. For two hours, I watched sharks and fish, noting relevant observations on a slate and checking the water temperature. Then, chilled after two hours in water that was 69°F, I was grateful to return to my own world, the shark club hanging from my belt in case of need. At two o'clock that afternoon, I went down for another two hours of observation while Manoel again chummed the water.

At the end of the first day, the sharks that appeared to be residents in my area and the many conventional fish that spent most of their time near the cliff face had become quite accustomed to the metal tube and its human occupant.

As we settled into our routines, I arranged with my topside crew to alter the timing of the chum drops, and I began experimenting with various substances to see what effect these might have upon the sharks. As I had already discovered elsewhere, I found that chunks of fresh fish elicited the most activity in the sharks as well as in the bony fish. During the beginning of my second week of observation, I took down a plastic bag full of fish chunks and released a few at a time into the water. The dozen or so sharks that were in attendance went into a feeding frenzy, despite the fact that whole fish were being tossed into the water by Manoel. The lumps of fish were definitely attractive!

During this madcap gang hysteria, a six-foot tiger shark appeared from deep water and killed and ate a dogfish, then struck a black-tip shark that I believed measured over three feet. The tiger, crazed by the scent and taste of the fish chunks, killed the black-tip, shook it, cut it in two and ingested the front half as I watched. This action took place about seven feet in front of my shelter. As the tail end of the black-tip began to sink, it attracted the attention of another tiger, this one only slightly smaller than the killer, but just as excited. Before the first tiger had swallowed his huge mouthful, the newcomer grabbed the rest of the black-tip and disappeared into the darkness below.

By now, all the pieces of fish had been eaten and the sharks began returning to more normal behavior, swimming in lazy circles or traveling upward or downward. Ten minutes later, the sea around me became peaceful.

Day by day, I became more absorbed in my research, yet I was always disappointed after each dive, for I had not sighted a really large shark, and particularly the great white, which was believed to be a frequent visitor on this side of the island. In the hope of meeting the white or another big shark of a different species, I had been holding back on my main experiments; but by the afternoon of day eleven, I was ready to give up waiting and to begin the tests that I felt would yield the greatest results.

The next morning the white shark turned up!

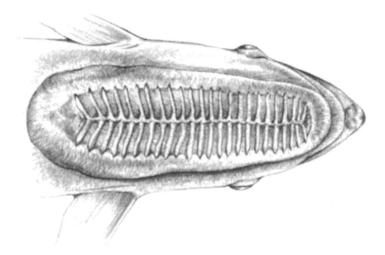

A DISC-LIKE STRUCTURE ON THE TOP OF A
REMORA'S HEAD ALLOWS IT TO ATTACH ITSELF TO
SHARKS AND OTHER LARGE FISH, GETTING A FREE RIDE
AND EATING FOOD THAT ESCAPES ITS CARRIER.

# Chapter 7

❧

AFTER THE white shark had eaten eight bass, he cruised around my area for some minutes. Evidently deciding that he had swallowed all that was easily obtainable, he moved away, appearing to be making for open water. When about ten minutes had elapsed, the lesser sharks began to reappear, a number of them cruising aimlessly some distance from my shelter and seen only as gliding shadows, others checking the surface and the area immediately around the tube, evidently searching for more handouts. Their behavior caused me to believe that the white had now gone; nevertheless, I waited another 15 minutes, just to be sure. At last, feeling really cold, I signalled topside, asking to be hoisted to the surface. I was thankful that the evening before I had asked Joaquim to raise the tube to the 20-foot level so that I could begin further tests the next day in better visibility. Should the big shark suddenly reappear, I now reasoned, I would not have far to go and wouldn't need to worry about decompression.

Just when I had eased myself out of the tube and closed the circular hatch, while I was still bending and looking downward, movement some distance beneath my feet attracted my attention. There was something down there, but it was too indistinct to recognize. Seconds later, as I was starting to rise, the white shark swam upward, coming into view in all its recognizable awesomeness about 40 feet ahead of the rock face. But it had its back to me and was going up at an angle.

My movement toward the surface seemed agonizingly slow. Carefully, so as to avoid scraping against the cliff and thus attracting the white's notice, I fended myself away from the rock with my left hand while I held the shark club ready in my right, willing myself meanwhile to remain calm. I had not been lifted more than a few feet when the shark turned full circle, its great head swinging from side to side in a manner that suggested it was preparing to attack. Now, I inadvertently stopped fending myself away from the rock. My helmet scraped against the rough surface, making a sound that was inordinately loud to my ears.

During these actions I had not taken my eyes off the shark for one instant, holding my stick up, ready to fend off the approaching monster. Then to my astonished relief, and just as my helmet grated against the rock for the second time, the great "killer" shark veered sharply to his right and streaked out of my vicinity with all appearances of panic! Seconds later, he was out of sight.

For many years, I have conditioned myself to remain calm during times of stressful inactivity, but I have never been able to maintain my cool *after* the fact. I don't collapse or fall apart emotionally, but I always react physically under the stimulus of a delayed adrenalin rush. At such times, my heart begins to beat at a slightly accelerated rate, my hands shake, my legs feel weak and my shoulder muscles become knotted. The cure, I have learned, depends on immediate physical activity.

As soon as I was relieved of helmet, air hose and lifeline, still attired in the diving suit and lead-weighted boots, I began tramping around on the rocky shore, trying to trot but accomplishing only a stumbling, slightly accelerated walk. Nevertheless, the energy needed to move myself while weighted down by my attire did the trick, burning off the excess adrenalin that had spurted into my blood while at the same time warming my chilled body. At the end of about five minutes, I had to sit down, panting and sweating, while Joaquim and Agostinho helped me out of the rubber suit.

My companions were puzzled by my strange behavior but too polite to ask the reason. Afterward, fully restored, I explained, whereupon Joaquim shrugged expressively.

*"No fais mal,"* he said, which is the Portuguese equivalent of "don't worry about it," which literally translated means "it makes no hurt." Afterward, he told me that, during the course of his diving activities, he had met several great white sharks; they had never tried to attack him and had usually fled the scene upon becoming aware of his presence. He went on to say:

"It's the small sharks I worry about. The little ones move about on the bottom, around rocks and dock pilings. Sometimes they may mistake the flash of a tool, like a knife or some other thing, for prey and they can attack. That's what happened both times I was bitten. And I've also had two strikes at my helmet and both sharks were small. I think that a hard-hat diver, because he moves so slowly and has those lines connected to the surface, either scares the big sharks or they don't mistake him for something that can be eaten."

When I went down the next day, I felt greatly reassured by Joaquim's views. Now I hoped the great shark would show up again, for I intended to make an important experiment and had brought along a razor blade and a bag of fish lymph expressly for the purpose. My intent was to test the shark's supposed liking for human blood, about which so much has been said in popular accounts. To do this, I proposed to cut one of my fingers with the razor blade (a small cut!), squeeze the digit intermittently to increase the flow of blood and wait for the results. Afterward, I would release fish lymph in the water and compare reactions. But I needed the white to be present, for this great fish was reputed to be the most blood-thirsty of all.

To encourage the sharks, I had bought an extra supply of fish from the islanders, and Manoel and Agostinho were to begin chumming the water when I signalled that I was inside the tube. Manuel worked from the 14-foot aluminum dinghy, Agostinho from the shore, and the lures were to be dropped at timed intervals.

My hope was that the white would turn up, but whether it did or not, I planned to go ahead with the experiment for I was now anxious to put my theories to the test. After long experience with predatory animals of many kinds, I was convinced that human blood is not in itself an attractant for any carnivore, despite the opinion of many. At the time of my work in Angola, I knew that carnivores such as wolves, lions and pumas did not attach much significance to the presence of human blood. At most, all of these land predators showed slight interest, but none ever sought to attack; neither did they become excited.

Even as I write this, I am caring for two wolves. As small pups, their sharp canines drew blood from me and my wife Sharon on a number of occasions, but every time I gave them an opportunity to scent, see and taste the fresh, warm blood, they sniffed indifferently and didn't even try to lick it. More recently, the female accidentally hit the back of my hand with one of her fangs, a sideways blow delivered as she moved her head quickly, which brought the canine into flat contact with my flesh. The tooth punched a hole that bled profusely. I offered the wound for the inspection of both wolves, but neither showed the slightest interest in it. Furthermore, it is our habit to give the wolves an early morning snack of raw beef chunks, which we take to their enclosure in a plastic dish, feeding them by hand. When the last morsels are gone, although I offer the bloody dish so that they may lick it, they ignore it in favor of leaping up to greet us, both paws on our shoulders.

After more than 30 years of field observation of animals, I have become convinced that five major factors induce carnivores to attack. The first is, of course, hunger; the second is defense of young; the third is defense of self; the fourth is defense of territory; and the fifth is defense of food. These are not listed in order of priority. The urge to attack is equally strong in each instance, although all predators attack most often in order to secure food because, quite simply, they are hungry with far greater regularity. In the case of sharks, however, one may safely eliminate the second factor — defense of young — for these fish are not protective of their offspring.

In a wild state, when a predatory animal sets out to hunt, it begins its search by using scent and hearing, the two most important senses in land animals that are equally important in sharks. But selachians are further aided by their lateral lines, which are sensitive to pressure changes, and by their acute electrical detectors, the ampullae of Lorenzini —

mucus-filled pits that are clustered around the snout and are capable of picking up electrical fields as weak as one five-thousandth of a microvolt per centimeter of body surface (one microvolt represents one millionth of a volt). This astonishing sensitivity allows sharks to locate prey even in pitch darkness when they detect the electrical emissions produced by all living things. In addition, sharks have other special sense endings on the outside of their bodies that can measure heat, cold, taste, touch and tension. Taken as a whole, these sensors make sharks the most efficient of all known predators.

Nevertheless, any hunter, no matter how sensitive it may be, cannot recognize as edible a scent, taste or sound issuing from a species that it has never before encountered. It is for this reason that man is not normally looked upon as prey by sharks.

Humans and all other animals emit many chemical, electrical and audible signals that are detectable at varying distances by sharks and other predators. When taken as a whole, these clues furnish a hunter with the identity of its natural prey; but because carnivorous animals, even sharks, are vulnerable when they attack large prey, they are usually cautious, for they know that if they are injured, their efficiency will be impaired and they may die of starvation or fall victim to another predator.

Sharks are far more interested in the combined signals given off by a potential prey animal than they are in individual scents, tastes or sounds. One isolated attractant, such as blood, does not provide enough information about the identity of a possible target, especially if it comes from a species that has never been encountered.

Man has long thought of predators as being blood-thirsty, but popular opinion notwithstanding, this belief is wrong. The only life-forms that can be considered truly blood-thirsty are the biting insects, some internal parasites and the vampire bats of Central and South America. All other predatory animals are, instead, *meat hungry*. Of course, blood is part of meat, but it is not sought for its own sake.

In view of these things, one might wonder why lymph proves so attractive to sharks, since it is contained within the body cavities and therefore would appear inaccessible before an injury is inflicted. A brief examination of this fluid, however, serves to explain the seeming contradiction.

Lymph is a slightly yellow, somewhat alkaline liquid similar to blood plasma that contains some white cells and is continuously drained from intercellular spaces by a network of minute tubes. It functions as a lubricant and at the same time carries away from the tissues unwanted materials such as excess hormones, some proteins, bacteria and other detritus. All of the waste products found in lymph eventually make their way to the outside of an animal's body, being voided through the skin (as sweat, for instance), in the urine or in the feces. These discharges give each species its own characteristic odor and taste. Predators, with their highly sensitive noses, can easily detect and follow their favored prey by locking onto the odor trails given off by the discharge of lymph, a process that is continuous in all species. But predators can also *taste* any substance that they can smell, for every scent is composed of a multitude of invisible particles that, once they are in contact with a predator's olfactory system, are immediately detectable by the taste buds. Thus, when lymph is used as a shark attractant, it acts as a sort of concentrated elixir far more potent and desirable than the small, diluted quantities given off by an animal during normal metabolism.

When I was preparing to conduct my tests off the Angolan island, I knew that a number of laboratory experiments had been made during which blood (from animals, not humans) and lymph had been offered to captive sharks. Lymph had never failed to produce aggression, but blood alone had yielded inconclusive results. Now, for my own satisfaction, I proposed to make the same tests in the shark's natural world. But I was going to use my own blood and fresh lymph from fish.

AT 11:00 O'CLOCK in the morning, the equatorial sun was nearing its noon zenith and casting brilliant light upon the surface of the water. Below, as I reached the tube, visibility was excellent, confirming the impression that I had formed while descending: there were sharks everywhere!

Attracted by the extra chumming, at least two dozen sharks of different species and sizes were competing for the handouts that were hitting the surface at regular but spaced intervals. So engrossed were the selachians that not one, not even an inquisitive black-tip, paid me the slightest notice. I spotted three makos, six small- to medium-sized tigers, several ragged-tooths between five and six feet long, black-tips and, lurking beneath their more powerful relatives, a veritable crowd of dogfish. But no white!

Wanting to prolong the baiting while supplies lasted, I now signalled an end to the chumming, especially in view of the fact that the sharks seemed about ready to go into a feeding frenzy. As the last of the gift fish were ingested and as the dogsharks and conventional fish were gulping down the morsels that had escaped the bigger predators, I settled myself within the tube, squatted on my seat and tried to determine the species and sizes of the sharks that I could see. Two of the makos were old friends, recognizable by a number of scars. One, the largest, had a badly ripped though healed dorsal. Another, a female, had bite marks on the narrow part of her body, about one foot ahead of the start of the tail fin. Several of the tigers also seemed familiar, but these were too far for me to be sure.

I was still trying to count and sort the sharks into their respective kinds when, as before, they all moved away. Was the white about to arrive? I started searching, peering alternately through each port, scanning the waters in front and below, but after several minutes of doing this without seeing more than the shadowy forms of some of the lesser sharks, I reluctantly decided that the others had moved off for some other reason.

At that moment a large, indistinct shape passed over the tube. Looking up, I saw the great shark almost immediately above me, only a few yards from the rock face. He was swimming practically on the surface, and I could see the wake created as his great dorsal cleaved through the surface. Now a veritable rain of dead fish splashed around the white. He turned lazily and began collecting the chum, swimming slowly toward each fish, opening his mouth slightly and sucking in the food. I signalled topside, asking that the chumming be stopped. When the last bait fish had been ingested by the white, I unwrapped the razor blade and made ready to test my theory.

Now I felt qualms! It was one thing to plan such a move in the sunshine of my own world, my body safe on the shore; it was quite another to put the plan into action when an enormous shark is cruising within 20 feet, a shark whose species has reportedly made the most attacks on humans and whose power is awesome!

Before descending, I had agreed with Joaquim that if the white became really aggressive, I would signal, at which point I would quickly be hauled up inside the tube. Now as I hesitated, razor blade poised over the little finger of my left hand, I realized that though I believed I was right in my calculations, I clearly had doubts, or else I lacked the courage to test my own convictions. This last thought put an end to my dithering. I sliced into the finger, feeling not the least pain despite the fact that I made a much deeper cut than I had intended.

The blood flowed freely. I held the finger just outside the center grill. It released a small, greenish red cloud near my shelter that became seized by the current and changed into tendrils. These drifted seaward, widening as they traveled and losing their color as the blood became thinned by the water.

The white shark had been aiming downward, traveling to the right as I cut my finger and pumped blood into the sea. Now he turned, moving his massive head from side to side, obviously reacting to the scent and taste of my blood within seconds of its release. Majestically, maintaining his unhurried rate of travel, he vectored on the trail, coming in the direction of the tube, but now that he was traveling toward the source of the blood, he no longer wagged his head.

Moments later I could see him clearly, approaching head-on, his mouth slightly open, revealing the lips and glimpses of the great teeth that were lying inward, in a state of repose. Seen from that angle, the great fish appeared to be smiling as he continued to make a leisurely approach. By the time he was about ten feet from my shelter, his calm demeanor had not changed; he was evidently somewhat curious, but not in the least excited. Then, as I began to fear he would actually bang his head against the center grill, he lost interest in the blood trail and turned from the island.

Soon after he moved away, the lesser fry began to arrive. The tiger sharks seemed most interested in the blood trail (I kept kneading the finger to maintain the flow), but not one of the sharks displayed even the mildest signs of frenzy. Two minutes later, I ended the experiment by slipping an elastic band around my finger to staunch the flow.

I had hoped that the white would remain in the vicinity for the second part of the experiment, but since he appeared to have gone, I picked up the bag of lymph and fish guts, undid its top and began squirting the contents through the port. In moments, bedlam erupted in the water around my shelter. Sharks came in from all angles, frantic, snapping at each other as they searched for the cause of the tantalizing scent-taste of the lymph. As I started to get worried because my tube was being repeatedly jostled by some of the larger sharks, the shape of the white became visible. It was approaching from my right.

Swimming faster than before, the enormous fish came straight in, reached me in seconds, was unable to turn swiftly enough to avoid a collision and crashed into the tube with part of his left side — a blow that jostled me and caused my shelter to crash into the rock, from where it bounced off and continued to swing violently. The momentum caused me to drop the bag of lymph to the floor of the tube. Now the *very* attractive contents spilled through the grill and caused a number of sharks, including one of the big makos, to attack from the bottom, bouncing my shelter. Meanwhile, the white had turned. He was coming in at speed. Frantically searching for the bag, I managed to grab it, ball it up and poke it through one of the grill openings. A four-foot tiger darted at it, champed on it and swam away, pursued by the white with the others following.

My theories were proven correct! This thought dominated as I clung to the sides of the tube and waited for it to settle back against the rock face. But I decided not to try the lymph stunt again; not from within my shelter, at any rate. Just then, what I wanted most of all was to return to my own environment, sip a glass of wine with my companions and let my stress dissipate in the sunshine. But first I had to make sure that the excitement was over, so I waited, watching the fish that were still darting around. Twenty minutes later, I gave the proper signal and was hauled up without mishap, my only companions being one black and white striped pilot fish, who either deserted the white shark or got left behind in the rush, and three small black-tips, without whose escort I would by now have felt lonely.

The pilot fish suggested by its behavior that it might have been contemplating switching allegiance from sharks to hard-hat divers! It kept swimming up to my helmet, descending along my body, poking curiously at the rubber suit before rising again to look at me through one of the three glass windows that were fitted into the helmet. This little fish, about ten inches long, was decorated by alternating black and white stripes, six of the former and five of the latter, the markings starting and ending with black. Members of the Carangidae, or caranx family, pilot fish are related to the horse mackerels, scads, jacks and pompanos.

The term "pilot fish" is misleading, for it is the shark that invariably chooses the route. It would be more accurate to call these fish *cleaners*, for it is evident that they accompany large sharks (or slow-moving vessels and driftwood logs) in order to make a living from the tiny organisms that often adhere to the rough skin of their hosts as well as to feast on the crumbs spilled after a shark makes a kill. The pilot fish that was inspecting me so carefully kept mouthing at the rubber suit, obviously checking to see if anything edible was sticking to the material, a task that occupied it until my head broke through the surface.

Following the human-blood/fish-lymph experiments under the surface, I began a series of tests in which I was assisted by Manoel and Agostinho, first using rags saturated in fish lymph and weighed with pebbles somewhat below the point of buoyancy. These were tossed into the water after I had stationed myself inside the tube. Only the first one or two were allowed to sink to a depth slightly below my observation shelter. Soon after the first traces of lymph provided scent-taste trails, the sharks came in, competing frantically for the privilege of ingesting the rags and stones. In all, two dozen of these decoys were thrown into the water during a one-hour interval. Every one was swallowed.

Next, using burlap, soft, fairly heavy wire and straw, we constructed a number of dummies resembling human figures. Manoel towed some of these on the surface in the dinghy at various speeds (none, however, faster than a human might be able to swim) and in various styles — zig-zagging, circling, straight, running and stop-and-go. These tests were made with the same dummy, which was never attacked, but from my shelter I was able to observe a number of sharks, especially tigers and makos, who rose to inspect the target. Nevertheless, none of these selachians went closer than about ten feet before turning away.

Again using the dummy but now weighted so that it would sink, Manoel towed it for some minutes, circling around the area of the rock face. The human effigy twisted and turned, legs and arms flapping slow-ly, at the ten-foot level. It lost the right leg when it almost hit an inquisi-tive mako. The shark, moving slowly and showing none of the aggressive actions compatible with the intention to attack, suddenly lashed at the dummy as it brushed by. It struck vigorously, shaking its head from side to side and shearing through burlap, straw and wire. Then it turned downward. Although I cannot be sure, it seemed that this attack was pre-cipitated by intrusion; that is to say, although the mako appeared to be curious, it only attacked when the straw "man" almost collided with it.

After that test, we started soaking the dummies in a variety of attrac-tants, including fish lymph, beef blood, human urine, dog feces — col-lected from the local inhabitants' dogs — chicken blood and guts and, the last experiment, my battery-powered electric razor, wrapped in plas-tic to make it waterproof and switched on.

All of these attractants prompted attacks. Indeed, we lost so many dummies that I at last abandoned the testing, for it was time-consuming to keep making them and rather expensive to buy burlap and wire, the cost of which rose in direct proportion to our need to purchase the ma-terial from the islanders.

The fish-lymph dummies (three of them) were promptly and vigor-ously attacked within moments of hitting the water. The first one was torn to shreds by two tigers, the second was converged on by an entire mob of mixed species, probably about a dozen in all. The action was so swift and confused that I could not tell which kind of shark struck first.

When things quieted down, all that remained of the dummy were a few strands of burlap and a cloud of drifting bits of straw.

During the third and last lymph test, the dummy was only lightly impregnated with the fluid. It sank to my own level, 20 feet, before the largest mako struck at it and tore it apart virtually in front of my eyes and only about a dozen yards away. Despite the fact I knew it was a dummy, the sight of its attack was so impressive that I felt horrified. Of course, at a distance of between 30 and 40 feet, I could not see detail, so the impression I received was that of a large shark attacking a swimming human, a most realistic experiment!

Human urine came in for a great deal of attention, although we only used one dummy upon which the four of us left our mark. It took longer for the sharks to pick up and follow the scent trail, but, led again by the feisty tigers, it was attacked and destroyed. Dog feces were next to arouse selachian enthusiasm, but drew an assembly of small sharks, most of which were dogfish. Beef blood was tentatively sampled by other small sharks, which snapped and slashed at the dummy but did not tear it apart; but chicken *blood and guts* created a lot of interest. That dummy was attacked by another mob, including two makos.

The last dummy tested contained my electric razor. Every shark in the vicinity became extremely excited within moments of the dummy being launched on the surface — in this case it was allowed to float on top, simulating a swimmer. From all quarters, a succession of sharks sped toward the dummy, which was very quickly pulled apart. I don't know which shark actually swallowed my razor, but one certainly did, for I had tied some loose, fluorescent ribbons to it and I did not see the package drop downward!

I would like to be able to say that I used my electric razor in this way because I suspected that sharks were able to detect electrical fields. The truth is that I knew nothing about this selachian ability at the time. Instead, I was curious to see if the persistent buzzing sound of the working razor would have an effect on the sharks, believing afterward that it must have been the rapid vibrations of the motor and rotors in the razor that drew attention to themselves. It is, of course, possible that the buzzing noise did have some effect on the sharks, but in view of the more recent findings, it is clear that the major attraction was the electrical fields put out by the razor.

Nevertheless, the results of those admittedly crude and often haphazard experiments that I conducted during my stay in Angola gave me a much better understanding of sharks and, more recently, when coupled with the latest findings, suggest an answer to a question that has caused considerable puzzlement: why is it that sharks rarely attack those people who so daringly go into the water to rescue a victim? If it is considered that human blood does not appear to cause much excitement among sharks and, demonstrably, does not draw other selachians to the locality of a strike, it seems logical to conclude that the attacking shark is not drawn to the large amounts of blood that surround victim *and* rescuers, but is instead locked onto the electrical fields of the victim.

It is well known that all activities in a vertebrate body are accompanied by electrical impulses. The human brain, for instance, produces a variety of electrical waves. The electroencephalograph has shown that when a human subject is resting quietly, eyes closed, electrical impulses known as alpha waves are produced at a rate of about ten per second; they have a measurable field of about 45 microvolts. These waves are wide and rhythmic, in contrast to the short, rapid waves that are emitted when an individual is excited. Hormones that induce and stimulate electrical waves in mammals include adrenalin, acetylcholine and serotonin — substances that are also exuded through the sweat glands onto the outside of the body.

Because of these things, I postulate that sharks are "tied" to their victims not because of outpourings of blood but because the stress induced by an attack produces higher electrical activity, which the attacker can easily detect, as well as increased body odors, also readily detected by a selachian's sensitive olfactory system. Thus, it is logical to assume that a terrorized victim has a higher output of electricity and body odors than do the rescuers, even though the latter must obviously be fearfully excited as well. As I noted during my Angolan experiments, the stronger the attractant, the more attention it received.

PERHAPS ONE of the most significant observations that I made during the
four weeks I studied sharks off the Angolan coast concerned the territorial competition that existed among sharks. This was entirely different to the way in which land animals relate to their range. On land, large
predatory animals live and hunt in a vast territory that they consider to
be their own and which they are prepared to defend against others of
their own kind. However, sharks, by virtue of the fact that they live in
the largest habitat to be found on earth — the oceans — where prey
species generally abound, are far less sedentary than their terrestrial
counterparts. With some exceptions, such as populations of reef sharks
that appear to patrol particular regions in a territorial way, most sharks,
especially the large ones, are migrants given to traveling wherever the
spirit moves them and, in some cases, traversing enormous distances over
a period of time.

Thus it appears that the majority of those sharks considered dangerous to man do not claim a large, geographical area of the submarine
world as their individual preserve. Instead, it seems that each shark has
what I call *personal space*, an area surrounding the animal into which no
intruder smaller than itself is allowed to trespass. In Angola and elsewhere, I observed countless instances in which smaller sharks that had
evidently strayed within the space of a large selachian were immediately
threatened, in some cases attacked and killed, although most trespassers
were quick to note the aggressive moves of the larger fish and even faster
to distance themselves from the aggressors. When this occurred, the
shark that had been encroached upon turned away from the interloper
once the latter had placed itself outside the invisible boundary that represented the aggressor's personal space.

This kind of territoriality is more common than unusual in the sea
and is practiced by most migratory fish, even within a school of the same
species. Anyone who has ever had an aquarium containing more than
one fish will know that one fish will threaten another when approached
closely by a companion, and the invader, if it is smaller, almost always
gives ground.

Land animals, including those that maintain well-defined ranges, also share the personal space taboo; so do humans, who will back away when an acquaintance steps too close to them. But in most cases, on land as well as in the ocean, the individual being encroached upon will either advertise its hostile intentions or simply retreat, preserving its personal space without having to fight. However, some land animals, notably grizzly bears, may well attack immediately if a human persists in advancing beyond the predetermined limit. Large sharks are especially prone to attack such invasions of privacy.

On land, it is difficult for an inexperienced person to determine whether or not an animal is reacting aggressively because it feels that its personal space is being encroached upon. But in the sea, it is absolutely *impossible* for surface swimmers to know if they are invading a shark's private domain. This is because bathers are rarely aware of the presence of sharks. In any event, if they do see a selachian in their immediate vicinity, there is nothing they can do to remove themselves from within its space quickly enough to avoid an attack.

All animals set their own highly individualistic spatial limits. What may be too close an approach for one shark or land animal may well be tolerated by another of the same species. In this context, divers have a better opportunity to determine whether or not they have trespassed — provided they actually see the shark — because these fish usually signal their aggressiveness. Most commonly, a selachian will begin to move its head and the fore part of its body from side to side in an agitated manner while humping its back — a display that may include one or more passes at the intruder. Nevertheless, most of the divers who have been attacked and who lived to tell about it reported that they had not been aware of the shark's presence until it had bitten them.

I am convinced that the majority of shark attacks upon humans have been motivated by territoriality. My view is supported by the International Shark Attack File, which shows that less than 20 percent of all attacks involved sharks that engaged in multiple strikes at their victims. In over 80 percent of the cases, selachians struck once, or at the most twice, and then left the scene. From these records, one may conclude that, having bitten a human, the sharks found they didn't like the taste, but this is not compatible with my own observations underwater and those of other observers.

Attacks caused by mistaken identity appear to have been made, however, but these have been aimed at divers wearing dark-hued or brightly colored wetsuits. Great whites, for instance, are known to prey on seals. A diver wearing a black garment and swimming underwater may well look like a seal to a hungry white. And the fashion-conscious divers who wear brightly hued suits may make targets of themselves because they are seen as rather interesting fish.

Undoubtedly, some sharks have attacked humans because they were hungry; these have eaten at least parts of the victim; in some grim cases, the victim has been swallowed whole. But such gruesome strikes appear to be the exception rather than the rule.

The French philosopher François Voltaire once said about a predator: "This animal is very vicious. When you attack him, he defends himself," in this way summing up humanity's approach to Nature — a double standard that permits man to commit all kinds of abominations against animals, but to act in horror when these "lower orders" fight back. Voltaire's succinct homily is particularly apt when applied to sharks. It is ironic that when a diver molests or actually attacks a shark and the latter retaliates by biting its tormentor, such a strike is recorded as an attack by the selachian against the human!

The Shark Attack File gives more than a few examples of such encounters, each case history showing that man was the aggressor and the sharks involved were merely defending themselves. Quite clearly, none of the divers would have been injured had they not opened hostilities. Similarly, when a fisherman catches a shark, becomes careless and is bitten by the fish — as was the case when Manolo exposed himself to the teeth of the small tiger — it is the man and not the selachian who should be blamed. For these reasons, at least as far as sharks are concerned, one may eliminate another factor that usually induces a predator to attack man. The fifth factor, defense of food, can also be eliminated, for only a raving lunatic would try to steal a selachian's natural prey right out of its mouth!

In sum, it seems evident that the great majority of strikes against humans have been induced by territorial defense and that the second and only other reason was hunger, sometimes involving divers who had speared fish and were towing their prizes on a line, spreading a tempting lymph trail.

Adding validity to the territorial defense theory is the fact that, in a number of attacks, the victims were not actually bitten but *raked* by the shark's upper teeth, which selachians can cause to be protruded by certain movements of the elastic upper jaw. These teeth are then used somewhat like swords. The shark charges the target and, when it reaches striking distance, swings its head to one side, then swings it back violently to bring the teeth into slashing contact with the victim's body and inflict major wounds. During such attacks, a shark may only strike once; on other occasions, the victim may be repeatedly raked before the attacker breaks off the engagement. Significantly, selachians that resort to this method of attack do not seek to eat the victim. Furthermore, this same kind of strike is used by sharks against others of their own or different species, as I have witnessed on several occasions. In all these observations, I can state with assurance that the slash strikes were directed at sharks that dared to swim too close to the attacker and that ignored the latter's warnings.

Giving further credence to the territorial theory is the fact that more than 80 percent of shark attack victims are likely to survive their injuries. This would not be the case if the attackers were motivated by hunger, for even a small shark can mutilate a victim beyond recovery.

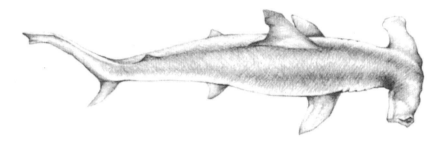

THE PURPOSE OF THE BIZARRE HEAD STRUCTURE
OF THE HAMMERHEAD SHARK CAN
ONLY BE GUESSED AT.

# Chapter 8

❧

FOSSIL SHARK TEETH that are very similar to but ten times larger than those of a great white shark are to be seen on exhibit in the Principality of Monaco's oceanographic museum. The teeth belonged to the monster that has been scientifically named *Carcharodon megalodon*. On the evidence of this giant's teeth, scientists have decided that it is the great white's nearest relative, or perhaps its progenitor. This selachian, which would have gulped down a man with little trouble, is thought to have become extinct in recent times. It would be good to know with certainty that this is so, but following an incident off Port Fairy, Australia, when a great white shark measured at 36½ feet became entangled in a heavy chain, and in view of a second sighting in Australia in 1918, when a gigantic white was seen after it had swallowed a number of crayfish traps, a few scientists argue that *Carcharodon megalodon* and *Carcharodon carcharias* are one and the same; that the giant shark whose huge teeth are on exhibit in Monaco may not be extinct at all; and that the great white sharks that are sometimes seen in the upper levels of the ocean, or patrolling inshore waters, are but *small* members of the species. According to this view, the *really* big whites may still exist in the deeps, where they feed on giant squid, whales and other large ocean dwellers.

Those who speculate about the existence of *C. megalodon* in today's seas cannot, of course, offer proof to back up their views; but those individuals who dismiss anything they cannot measure and document in accordance with the principles of scientific dogma would do well to remember the words of Charles Elton, the eminent British biologist. In his book *Animal Ecology* (Macmillan, New York, 1927), he wrote that Darwin's discoveries "had the remarkable effect of sending the whole zoological world flocking indoors, where they remained hard at work for fifty years or more, and whence they are now beginning to put forth cautious heads again into the open air." Similarly, another forward-thinking British biologist, Thomas Henry Huxley (1825-95), said that scientific thought is nothing more or less than common sense well regulated.

Common sense implies the use of logic, deduction and the intuitive leap, all of which are becoming scarce in many scientific cloisters because far too many biologists are ultrasensitive to the criticism of their peers (often too freely and too negatively given). This means that an investigator who dares to think contrary to the accepted dogma will hesitate to advance an opinion that is not backed up by multiple references citing the work of other scientists as well as by years of research and experimentation.

During the first half of this century, many scientists ignored the view of both Huxley and Elton, convinced that life could not exist in the deep ocean because the enormous pressure encountered there would crush any living thing. Such a view was more compatible with the thinking of an untutored landsman. We know today that a large variety of animals, large and small, make their home in the deeps. We also know that the evidence we have applies only to minuscule areas of the ocean. As one oceanographer put it recently, experiments undertaken so far in the deep seas can be compared to an attempt to determine the oil-bearing capacity of the entire state of Texas by drilling only one test hole.

Although several great white sharks have been found that exceed the length of the 21-foot white, now considered the largest of its kind, the scientific literature does not acknowledge that at least one *Carcharodon carcharias* was 15½ feet longer than the official record holder. Instead, hedging, the literature states that great whites longer than 21 feet *may* be found in the ocean. Such a caveat would be more balanced if it was also stated that the shark found off the coast of Australia was said to have attained a length of 36½ feet. Similarly, a great white harpooned off the Azores Islands in 1981, which measured 29 feet 3 inches long, has not yet been either confirmed or denied by the experts.

There can be little doubt that the ocean deeps could easily support giant sharks, for those nether worlds offer an enormity of space in which plenty of food is to be found. Those enormous carnivores, the sperm whales, which can reach a length of at least 60 feet and attain a weight of more than 120,000 pounds, obtain their food in the Stygian abyss. If a whale, which must rise to the surface in order to breathe, can obtain food in those great deeps during the space of 90 to 120 minutes, a shark can store energy in its liver and remain in the deeps during its entire lifetime.

Those who hypothesize that *megalodon* and *carcharias* may be one and the same species, slightly altered by evolution from an ancestral prototype, suggest a scenario in which the really large sharks usually remain in the deeps, rarely rising to seek food elsewhere; whereas the young and intermediate-sized whites hunt the upper levels of ocean until they attain sufficient size to compete in the world of their giant kin.

Although it has been established that whites are ovoviviparous, little else is known about the reproductive biology of these sharks due to the fact that pregnant females have only rarely been taken. It is believed that females become sexually mature when they reach a length of about 14 feet. It is also believed that pup whites are born when they are about four feet long. Such speculation, because it has been included in the scientific literature, is widely accepted despite the fact that it is not supported by scientifically acceptable proof. Yet data that has not been officially recognized by scientific literature is cast aside. Such a double standard leaves me baffled! If it is considered "good biology" to accept such unsupported conclusions, why is it not acceptable to mention that the sizes of a number of great whites caught and measured by experienced laymen greatly exceed the 21-foot record? Any why is it unscientific to speculate about the continued existence of *Carcharodon megalodon*?

The ocean, which is the last frontier of our planet, is an environment shrouded in mystery, despite the knowledge accumulated particularly in recent times. As a result of modern research, it is now known that the great deeps abound with life, but those organisms so far discovered probably represent only a minute percentage of the animals that make their home down there in the bowels of the earth.

The sea has given man tantalizing and astonishing revelations. One of these, in 1976, was the accidental discovery of a shark, which was not even suspected. Termed Megamouth, this selachian represents not only a new species but a completely unknown family.

Megamouth, a male that was 15 feet long and weighed 1,600 pounds, became entangled in a parachute-type sea anchor deployed by a United States naval vessel off the island of Oahu, Hawaii. This bizarre creature attempted to swallow the large orange and white parachute. The anchor was down to the 500-foot level when the shark tried to eat it, and it died as a result.

Similar to the whale and basking sharks, this new fish has a terminal mouth of gigantic proportions that is studded with rows of sharp, backward-sloping teeth. It has prominent, fleshy-looking lips, a domed head, two fairly small dorsal fins, long and relatively narrow pectoral fins and a caudal fin, or tail fin, with an upper lobe that is considerably longer than the lower extremity of this forked organ. It is believed that this shark, like the whale and basking species, also feeds on planktonic organisms, although its mouth is far bigger and its gill slits are smaller.

Before the American Navy discovered Megamouth, the captain and crew of another of its ships, the *USS Stein* — a frigate that left San Diego to patrol South American waters — got a different kind of surprise from another deep-dwelling organism. This one, however, was never seen, but it left some of its teeth stuck in the warship's sonar dome. As a result, the ship's sound-locating gear became unserviceable, and the captain returned to port.

In dry dock, the tough, rubberized coating that protected the underwater dome was found to have been torn by some sort of marine dweller, which had left behind dozens of hollow, sharp teeth, some of which were more than an inch long. Whatever had been drawn to attack the dome was presumed to have been huge and of an unknown species.

Long before these contemporary events, however, the sea had produced other bizarre creatures. In the latter part of the nineteenth century, in the Bay of Bengal, India, a gigantic squid was reported to have attacked a 150-ton sailing ship, the *Pearl*. This happening was witnessed by the crew of a British steamship, the *SS Strathowen*, who swore that they saw giant tentacles pull the ship over. All hands are reported to have been lost.

Not long after that display of monstrous strength, the remains of a gigantic sea creature were washed ashore at St. Augustine's Beach, Florida, in 1896. This story, however, did not end until 1971!

The unceremonious arrival of a huge and rotting mound of ocean dweller on the Florida beach reached the ears of DeWitt Webb, a member of the local Scientific and Historical Society, who contacted Professor W. H. Dall of the National Museum in Washington, D.C. Dr. Webb noted that the partial carcass "must have weighed six or seven tons." He wrote that it took six men, four horses and much tackle to move the animal's remains 40 feet higher up the beach. The vast mound of decomposing tissue was said to measure 21 feet across and 7 feet thick, with skin 3½ inches thick. Dr. Webb sent some samples to Washington, where they were examined and said to belong to a whale. Parts of these samples were later sent to the Smithsonian Institution, where they were stored in preservative and forgotten until two scientists found them in 1971. After their examination of the tissue, these biologists became satisfied that it did not belong to a whale but to an octopus of gigantic proportions.

In 1915, the sea sent up another monster. This time, during World War I, the animal came to the surface on July 30 after a German submarine, the U28, commanded by Captain Georg vonVorstner, had torpedoed the British *SS Iberian* in the Atlantic Ocean. Reporting the matter, the U-boat commander gave this account:

"The steamer sank quickly. When it had been gone for about twenty-five seconds, there was a violent explosion. A little time later parts of the wreck, among them a gigantic sea animal, writhing and struggling wildly, were shot out of the water up to a height of between sixty and a hundred feet. . . I had with me in the conning tower the chief engineer, the navigator and the helmsman. We did not have time to take a photograph. The animal sank out of sight after about ten or fifteen seconds. It was about sixty feet long, a crocodile in shape and had four limbs, powerful, webbed feet, and a long tail that tapered to a point."

Unlike the tangible evidence supplied by Megamouth, the teeth in the sonar dome and the remains washed ashore at St. Augustine, Captain von Vorstner's monster left no physical part of itself that could be scientifically examined. History records its presence, as it does the squid that toppled the schooner in the Bay of Bengal, but all we have are the words of the observers. It can be argued that the crew of the British *Strathowen* were unreliable witnesses and that, in any event, too much time has passed since the tragedy to allow for checking. But it is hardly possible to say the same of a U-boat captain and his three crew members, all experienced sailors and observers who were duty-bound to keep a meticulous log. Similarly, the report concerning another washed-up carcass, this time found in southwest Scotland, cannot be doubted, despite the fact that the giant remains were not scientifically examined.

In the summer of 1942, residents of the town of Gourock, on the River Clyde, began complaining of a dreadful smell that was invading their homes. The number of complaints was sufficient enough for the local government to ask one of its officials, Councilman Charles Rankin, to investigate the source of this pestilence. The Clyde, which drains the surrounding counties of Renfrew, Dunbarton, Stirling and Lanark, joins its fresh waters with those of the Atlantic in an arm of the ocean that gives access to the Firth of Clyde, a dogleg-shaped bay that lies between the coast of Ayrshire and the Island of Arran. Gourock, on Renfrew's northwest tip, is situated on a coastline. Its waters are more salt than fresh, since it is less than 20 miles from the opening to the Firth of Clyde.

Rankin and the town's public works foreman went down to the shore to investigate and were confronted by the rotting carcass of a very odd beast. It was 28 feet long and 6 feet deep at the area of greatest girth. Rankin later reported:

"As it lay on its side, the body seemed to be oval, but the angle of the flippers in relation to the animal's size suggested that it had been round in life. The head, neck, body and tail were equally long, the neck and tail gradually tapering away from the body, but there were no fins.

"At the front of the body there was a pair of L-shaped flippers and a similar pair at the back. But these were shorter and wider. The flippers were like the tail, with the gristly bones that looked as if they would open like a fan."

Rankin also said that the body was sparsely covered with hard, bristlelike hairs that were about six inches long. He plucked one of these. Later after it had dried, this hair coiled up like a watch spring.

Charles Rankin tried to interest Scotland's Royal Museum without success; then he tried to photograph it, but he was forbidden to do so because, at the height of the war, the area had been restricted. In the end, the carcass was buried, but not before Rankin had done a bit of dissecting on his own, discovering that, although the skin was thin, it was elastic and tough. The flesh, he said, was pinkish but blubbery. It was difficult to cut. The only recognizable object found in the stomach was a piece of tasseled tablecloth.

From Rankin's description of the Gourock Monster, it is clear that the animal was neither shark nor whale but seemed to have characteristics of both. It would be fascinating to dig up the remains, providing the bones have endured. But this is unlikely, for if the bones were composed of cartilage, they have probably decomposed by now.

In his book *The Kon-Tiki Expedition,* Thor Heyerdahl discusses deep-sea monsters, including large squid that would surface at night, evidently attracted by the raft's lantern, and would remain on the surface, staring out of huge, round eyes. Indeed, Heyerdahl was warned by Peruvians before he left South America that there was danger from giant squid that could drag a man off the craft. This did not happen to the daring explorer and his crew, but it did happen to one sailor, again during World War II.

After their ship was sunk by a German surface craft, 12 British sailors saved themselves by climbing on board a life raft. Included in the party were three lieutenants, Cox, Davidson and Rolandson. Since there was no room on board the raft for all the survivors, some clung to the sides. A number of these were attacked and killed by sharks, but after several days, the selachians disappeared. Shortly afterward, an enormous squid surfaced beside the men, shot out one massive tentacle and grabbed one of the sailors. Lieutenant Cox and his companions tried to save the man, but the squid dragged him off and submerged with him. Cox received a number of sucker marks. The men were rescued by a passing ship the next day.

There are many mysteries in the ocean, and sightings of strange animals will occur from time to time. It is hoped that science will not dismiss these. Recent discoveries in the Galápagos Rift, west of Ecuador, have proved that, no matter how bizarre an event may seem to us who dwell on land, it might be a commonplace happening in the ocean!

Intrigued by evidence gathered in the Galápagos Rift area by the Scripps Institution of Oceanography, Oregon State University and Woods Hole Oceanographic Institution, 25 scientists and 26 technicians sailed for the Galápagos in 1976 in the research ship *Knorr*, an expedition sponsored by the National Science Foundation of the United States as part of the International Decade of Ocean Exploration. The earlier oceanic probe had detected mounds created by hydrothermal vents caused by heat and gases escaping from beneath the earth.

In February 1977, the *Knorr* team took water temperatures. At a given location, about one and a half miles down, the near-freezing water of the winter ocean began to warm up. Photographs then revealed thousands of giant clams of a kind never before seen. Later, diving in the minisub *Alvin*, the scientists discovered not only a number of new organisms, including giant tube worms, but a world in which all life depended for survival not on oxygen but on hydrogen sulphide, a poison first utilized by bacteria that, in turn, were eaten by other tiny organisms that were ingested by bigger animals. This was a staggering discovery! Until that moment, it had been universally thought that nothing could survive in the absence of oxygen; but down there in the Galápagos Rift, life was thriving not only on what was considered poison but in water that within the radius of the vents was heated to 350°C (650°F). According to scientific norms, what those investigators discovered was simply not possible. But it was there!

Reports of these discoveries were carried by *National Geographic* in its October 1977 and November 1979 issues. They may be especially interesting to skeptics who persist in clinging to ultratraditional dogmas of science.

Now that the impossible has been scientifically proven to be possible, the big question is: *what else is down there?*

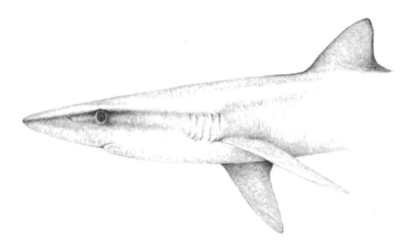

THE BLUE SHARK REACHES LENGTHS OF
12 TO 15 FEET, OCCASIONALLY 25 FEET.
ITS AVERAGE WEIGHT IS 550 POUNDS

# Chapter 9

✤

DURING THE summer of 1932, when I was almost 11 years old, I saw a sea monster. So did hundreds of other bathers on the beach just outside of Palma de Mallorca. The creature was an octopus, but it was enormous; and for reasons unknown, it decided to walk up the shingle, first becoming visible as a round, grayish dome that rose out of the Mediterranean about 30 feet from shore. Soon the eyes came into view, staring, round shiny orbs slightly smaller than the mouth of a teacup. By now, people were scrambling out of the water, attracting the notice of a pair of patrol policemen, members of Spain's national police, the *Guardia Civil*. By the time these lawmen reached the shoreline, the creature's tentacles were half out of the water. It was literally walking on the sand, each of its eight arms forming an **S**-bend as it moved. At this stage, everybody was standing on land. One of the policemen lifted his rifle and shot the octopus, placing a bullet between its eyes. The animal convulsed, squirted great clouds of dark-brown ink, thrashed the water with its arms, then became still. It was dead.

Later examination determined that this was the largest member of its kind ever to come out of the Mediterranean Sea.

Although I was greatly impressed at the time, I know today that this Cephalopoda was not of record size — 20-footers that weigh 150 pounds can be found in the Straits of Georgia off the coasts of the State of Washington and British Columbia — but none of the witnesses of the Mallorca event could ever have been convinced that they had not seen a veritable marine monster. The pity of it is that the animal was cut into pieces by various people (I helped, taking home the eyes!) and so no one will ever know what it was that caused the animal to behave so untypically. Normally shy and retiring, octopuses do not, as a rule, leave their underwater habitats, nor do they usually even rise to the surface. In any event, the why of it all must go unanswered, although it may be that my boyhood monster was sick, perhaps disoriented because of pollution or some other affliction.

As might have been expected, the beach drew hundreds of curious people who came daily in the hopes of seeing another monster octopus, but the water remained empty of swimmers. Of course, no other apparitions rewarded the curious, and eventually the tenor of beach life returned to normal.

That incident was an important one for me. After I had sent a photograph of the creature home to my father, he sent it to one of the daily newspapers in my hometown. It was published and I got my very first byline! My interest in nature was fanned into a passion by that taste of fame; and ever since, I have been keeping my eyes open for other monsters!

For a brief time in 1971, I was sure I had at last discovered a truly gigantic and unknown marine monster. I was conning the *Stella Maris* into the open Pacific in the area between the Queen Charlotte Islands and Vancouver Island, in Queen Charlotte Sound, when I spotted what I first thought might be the wreckage of a vessel. Putting on speed, I headed for the indistinct mass that rose and fell as it responded to the Pacific swells. As I drew nearer, and perhaps because my last landfall had been Ness Point on the British Columbia mainland, I believed I was on the track of a major discovery.

Through my field glasses I became convinced that I was watching a 60-foot creature that was moving in a snakelike manner, showing four large humps as it slithered through the water. I set the engine at full ahead, locked the wheel and grabbed for my camera, but before I could lean out of the cockpit to begin to focus, my monster split in two, and I soon realized I had stumbled on two basking sharks swimming in tandem. Undaunted, I sped on, intending to take pictures of the baskers, but they dived before I was in range. Soon afterward, they reappeared again, farther out to sea, and I tried once more.

The basking shark is the second largest selachian presently recognized, obtaining a length between 35 and 40 feet. Like the whale shark, it also feeds on planktonic organisms and is harmless — unless, of course, an incautious sailor puts his small boat within reach of a slap from the powerful tail.

These were the only basking sharks I have ever seen, but they reminded me of events in Angola, when I was preparing for a night dive under full moon and Joaquim arrived in the morning to announce that a commercial fishing vessel had sighted four basking sharks about 60 miles from Luanda. Knowing that these selachians are thought to spend the winter in hibernation, probably in relatively warm water and close to shore, Joaquim thought there might be an outside chance of seeing one of these creatures, especially during a night dive. I was not so sanguine, for I felt that the odds of being present to witness a basking shark were too great for contemplation. I was correct in this view, for no basker came near my tube, though other selachians did.

The moon was full at 11:00 p.m., a great, pinkish dish shining out of a cloudless sky. Already dressed, I had waited until the night light had risen full in the sky, wanting to get as much of its refulgence as possible. I sat on the rock, feet dangling in the water, and wriggled forward as Joaquim and Agostinho helped me. Soon I was under the water and at first captivated by the splendor that surrounded me. I was in a silver-green world filled with fluorescent particles. Plankton, small fish, large fish at a distance, more spectral glows in the deeps ahead . . . lights all over the place, some intense green, others faint glows, like wet phosphorus. Some drifted with the currents, many darted about. The spectacles were numerous and splendid.

Guided by the hoist cable. I slid downward. Soon my feet touched the top of my shelter. At that moment, I saw a large, faintly glowing shape approaching from the bottom. Without seeing more than the vaguely luminous, indistinct aura, I knew it was a large shark, and this awareness caused me to realize how helpless and vulnerable man is when he invades the night world of the selachians. I had dived at night before this time, sometimes wearing scuba gear, but more frequently free of equipment. Invariably, although I was always enchanted with the Cimmerian ocean, I was also uncomfortably aware of my inability to compete sensorially with its inhabitants. I had felt somewhat the same when I first set out to explore the night forest, but in that terrestrial milieu, my faculties served me reasonably well once I learned to sharpen them and to properly interpret the environmental messages they gathered. In the forest I can hear, smell and see, even if all my senses are poor compared with those of any forest dweller. In the forest, I can also breathe unaided and move about freely and surely. But in the moonlit sea, without artificial illumination, hearing is useless, scent is nonexistent and vision is minimal — even with goggles — and restricted to a few yards in any direction.

It is possible to pick up vague detail during a moonlight dive, but range is cut down drastically when one looks downward, to the sides or ahead. Only when scanning the surface is it possible to pick out more distant objects, but these are noted as silhouettes. Light, of course, is visible whether caused artificially, through the bioluminescence of animals or by moonshine, but it is diffuse, rather like the glow cast by a street lamp in heavy fog. Hindered by the cumbersome diving helmet, I felt even more helpless as I reached for the hatch cover while trying to identify the kind and size of shark that was coming toward me.

Before deciding to make that night dive into waters in which sharks virtually abounded, I had been perfectly aware that I was exposing myself to possible attack. But because I felt that my research would not be complete without such an experience, I went ahead despite Joaquim's protestations. He knew, as I did, that conditions after sunset are all in favor of the sharks, and that these superb predators are then much more aggressive. But I felt it was important to go down aided only by the light of the moon so that I could observe the nighttime behavior of selachians and compare it to their daylight activities and moods. I also wanted to explore the problems one must encounter during such an activity so that I might better understand the helplessness of humans who, wittingly or otherwise, find themselves exposed to the darkened sea. None of my previous night dives could be compared to this one because, during all of the former, I had not deliberately sought to attract sharks to my area of operations. Selachians had no doubt been present, as they are in any part of the ocean, but they had not been encouraged to congregate in one place.

Now, as I slipped into my shelter and quickly closed the hatch, I realized for the first time just how great the risk was to which I had exposed myself. I had not yet fastened the latch that secured the lid when the phosphorescent shark that I had been watching charged the top part of the tube. The collision, like that of the white, caused my shelter to swing wildly and to scrape and bang against the rock face.

While this was happening, I was unable to see anything outside of the tube, but as the momentum slackened and I steadied myself on the jump seat, I looked out of the central port in time to see that the shark was coming back. I could not distinguish its details, yet I noticed that it was swinging its head and forequarters from side to side. Its intentions were clear: it was coming to attack again. Seconds later, it hit the mesh of the central port, inches from my face. I saw teeth break out of the jaws and sink downward almost at the moment that my shelter began to bounce and swing anew. This time, however, it was not given time to settle before the shark charged again, but I was too busy hanging onto the mesh lid to notice where the brute impacted against the metal.

Releasing the mesh with one hand, I jerked the signal rope, but it was not until I felt myself being pulled up against the closed hatch that I realized I had asked to be lifted out of the tube and up to the surface. Frantically, I pulled the rope again, but it was too tight to register the tugs topside. Now, as my shelter was hit again, I resisted the pull of Manoel and Agostinho, hoping to get some slack. They had already noticed from my resistance that something was wrong, and they slackened the rope. At last I gave the correct number of pulls and felt the tube move, but not before the frenzied shark struck yet again.

Since the tube was at the 20-foot level, it did not take long to reach the surface. Even so, the shark followed, twice biting at the bottom of the tube. When about a third of the tube was out of the water and in the blessed light of two large carbide lanterns, I lifted the lid, but it was not until I had been helped onshore that I learned that the shark had surfaced nearby, almost at the same moment that my shelter cleared the water.

I had been unable to determine the shark's identity or even to make a guess as to its size, although it must have been in excess of ten feet. My companions, who saw its great dorsal fin when it cleared the water, were to argue interminably about its species. Joaquim was sure it was a blue shark, Manoel voted for the white and Agostinho insisted it was a mako. I let them argue while I thought about the experience, then vowed never again to seek such an encounter.

THE MOONLIGHT DIVE brought to conclusion my research in Angola. It had not accomplished what I had hoped for, but it caused me to think hard about the reasons underlying shark frenzy. Today, I still cannot be sure about my conclusions, but logic suggested a possible explanation. Considering a shark's fine-tuned nervous system, as well as the many sensorial aids that keep it in constant touch with its environment, it occurred to me one day that there was a grim similarity between a group of frenzied sharks and a human lynch mob. Both species, man and shark, appear to be easily influenced by the phenomenon of crowd hysteria. The shark is driven to frenzy not so much by hunger as by competitors of its own kind; but it only behaves abnormally when food stimulates its appetite and prepares it for aggressive behavior. In this state, the nearness of other sharks, each equally stimulated and all emitting heightened electrical fields, produces hysteria. The madness begins, intensifies because of competition and does not end until the cause, or trigger, has been destroyed, or eaten.

While being bounced inside my tube by that furious Angolan shark, I had no time to think abut how I could defend myself if I were spilled out of it. Later, I pondered the matter and formed some conclusions that might have helped me stay alive. After reading the Shark Attack File, I learned that my thinking coincided with the conclusions formed by a number of researchers.

The first thing that should be done by an individual who is either threatened or attacked is the most difficult: remain calm. At least one victim struck by a white shark did nothing. By playing dead, it seems, the shark was satisfied and let the man go. This strongly suggests that the strike was territorially motivated.

If a shark is not signalling aggression, a swimmer should not resort to threatening movements. The shark may only be curious; it may have no intention of striking unless it feels threatened by the human. In such circumstances, the selachian might retreat before a sudden and aggressive move, but it could attack in self-defense. Faced by a curious selachian, the best thing to do is to try to get ashore quickly without exhibiting either panic or undue haste; or, if diving, seek shelter under the water against rocks or in a cave; attempt to get back to the dive boat as soon as possible. Conversely, if a shark comes within arm's length, it might be wise to strike at it.

In 1972, while diving in the Pacific off the coast of British Columbia, an eight-foot blue shark came visiting. Although it did not show outward signs of aggression, it began to make passes, swimming closer and closer with each one. During its last approach, it was so close that I was able to literally punch it on the nose with my balled fist. That caused it to back away, but it followed me as I moved along a rock cliff toward the place where my boat was anchored. Although I cannot be sure, I believe it was the *Stella's* slowly swaying anchor rope that caused the shark to go away.

The most sensitive parts of a shark are its gills and eyes. A number of victims have saved themselves by attacking those organs. Similarly, victims have saved themselves by kicking at the shark or even punching it. If a victim succeeds in causing the shark to let go and to cease attacking, then the two most important things are: try to stop the bleeding; get to shore as quickly as possible.

Since man is so helpless against sharks, it is clear that prevention is far more effective than defense. Although I must plead guilty of not practicing what I preach, it is undoubtedly potentially dangerous to swim alone and therefore safer to swim with a friend and remain reasonably near other bathers. Then, too, if one knows that a particular area is frequented by sharks, it should be avoided. It is also good to remember that the farther from shore, the greater the likelihood of encountering large sharks and the less chance there is of rescue.

Night swimming and diving is dangerous in any waters warm enough for human use. The same holds true of waters that are murky or roiled up by crowds of bathers.

Beaches with groups of exceptionally noisy bathers should be avoided, for such commotion may attract sharks. The same is true of people who resort to horseplay in the shallows, such as splashing, making screeching sounds with compressed lips at water level or generally jumping about. All of these things produce pressure waves that may interest hunting sharks.

It should not be necessary to state this, but unfortunately it is: Bathers and swimmers should not use the sea as a repository for their personal wastes; these substances attract sharks!

Buckles, bracelets, medallions or shiny objects should not be worn. Similarly, gaudy, bright swimwear should be avoided, as well as black. In-between, nonfluorescent shades are less likely to attract sharks.

There are other precautions that may be taken, all of them basic common sense. One should not molest sharks, even the smallest; one should not tow dead fish through the water; one should not surf on brightly colored or black boards; one should avoid sudden drop-offs, where sharks might lurk; one should check reefs and sandbars during low tides, for sometimes a shark may be cut off from the open sea by the receding water. My advice to anyone using the sea is to enjoy it while being sensible. The chances of attack in most waters are *infinitesimal.*

Until a repellent is available that is sure to work on all species of sharks, it is advisable to behave cautiously and sensibly. A number of such products are on the market, but their reliability should not be counted on. More recently, tests of a substance emitted by a fish, the lemon sole, have proven interesting. Sharks avoid biting this fish; and if a synthetic substitute can be found that is effective, perhaps man will be able to swim with relative impunity.

Considering the millions of swimmers who use the sea worldwide, the percentage of attacks is very small. More people are killed or injured on the highways of the world in one week than are likely to be attacked by sharks in ten years.

Despite their potential for mayhem, sharks as a whole are fascinating, wonderfully adapted animals that offer a great many benefits to mankind. Their flesh is eaten worldwide and is the mainstay of the populace in some countries. Their livers yield huge quantities of oil and vitamins. A substance called squalene that is found in the livers of deep-sea sharks has multiple uses: it does not freeze and so is employed as a lubricant in high-flying aircraft. It is now also being used in the treatment of burns; and chances are that ladies who use lipstick are applying squalene to their lips or using it in other forms of makeup.

Another substance known as coenzyme Q10 is being tested medically as a cure for cancer. In addition, shark skin is tanned into thin but durable leather; as shagreen it is used to sand down fine woods; shark spinal columns are dried, polished and fashioned into walking sticks and other ornaments, and even the teeth are used as jewelery.

A shark, whatever its species, is a fascinating animal that may yet teach humans a great deal about the biology of our planet.

# AFTERWORD
# *The Biology of Sharks*

❦

A S FAR AS science can determine, today's sharks have existed for about 350 million years and may well have been swimming in the seas of our world, relatively unchanged, for a good deal longer than that. As has already been noted, it is even possible that the giant of them all, *Carcharodon megalodon,* could still be swimming in the great deeps of the ocean.

From fossil teeth that are almost as large as a man's open hand, it has been deduced that *megalodon* attained a length of at least 80 feet. Also from its teeth it has been determined that this, the largest known marine predator, was the direct ancestor of the great white shark, *Carcharodon carcharias,* the species that, if its giant near-relative really is extinct, is the biggest of all present-day predatory sharks.

Most writers — and hence most people — speak about sharks in the singular, a habit that has led to much misunderstanding because it lumps together some 350 species of marine animals and obscures the essential differences that exist between them. It would be as wrong to speak of "the bird" when discussing the avian species in general; or to talk about "the mammal" without reference to individual types — one of which, of course, is our own!

Sharks belong to the class Selachii, which also includes rays, skates, sawfishes, guitarfishes and ratfishes. All of them share one special physical characteristic: their skeletons are made of cartilage, or gristle, rather than of bone. Sharks, skates and rays have been grouped into one

...class, the Euselachii, then separated into two orders, the Pleuro-
tremata: sharks; and the Hypotremata: skates and rays. The classification
in each case is further divided into suborders, families, species and sub-
species, according to a system first published in 1735 by the Swedish
naturalist Carl von Linne, or Linnaeus, as he became known. But the
common name used by English-speaking people and applied generally to
all selachians has no such scientific root. Indeed, the term was not used
until the last part of the fifteenth century and is believed to owe its origin to the German word *schurke*, meaning villain. However this may be,
sharks represent somewhat less than one percent of a total of about
40,000 fish and fishlike animals that live in the ocean.

Until the late 1960s, only about 250 kinds of selachians had been
identified; but with the advantage of modern underwater equipment and
more liberal funding of oceanographic research, nearly 100 new species
have since been recorded — and it is likely that even more hitherto
unknown sharks will be discovered before another decade is spent.

Sharks of one sort or another inhabit all the oceans of the world,
from tropical to cold northern regions; and although it seems that some
of the large dangerous kinds prefer warm seas, even these are often found
in coastal areas where the water is only a few degrees above freezing during the winter. This is not surprising, however, because sharks are known
to descend to great depths, where year-round temperatures range between
33° and 36°F.

The whale shark is the largest of all the presently identified species,
but this giant feeds almost exclusively on marine plankton, tiny animals
and larva that are strained out of the water by much the same method
used by whales. This shark is believed to reach 60 feet in length and to
weigh 17 tons; other more conservative estimates put its maximum
length at 50 feet and its weight at 15 tons. The next largest, also a plankton feeder, is the basking shark, said to reach 45 feet and to weigh several
tons. Both of these giants, and the rather bizarre Megamouth, are considered harmless; they are not thought to be true predators and have
never been known to attack humans. All other sharks are predatory.
They seek out, chase and kill their prey. The smallest of these is a little

selachian called *Etmopterus*, which at full maturity seldom exceeds one foot in length.

About one third of all female sharks lay eggs in the area of weed beds, the remainder give birth to live young; their embryos develop in twin wombs without benefit of a placenta or any other connection to the mother's blood supply — a peculiarity that places these selachians in a category between mammals and egg layers. (The mammalian placenta is an organ formed in the lining of the mother's uterus by a union between the uterine membrane and the membranes of the fetus. This provides the growing embryo with nourishment and eliminates its wastes through the female's own excretory system. Animals hatched from eggs outside of a female's body, in contrast, feed on the yolk and void their wastes inside the shells, which may be hard as that of a chicken, soft and gelatinous as those of fish and amphibians, or leathery as those of sharks and turtles.) Whether they develop inside a womb or within a tough egg case attached to an undersea weed bed, all young selachians must take care of themselves from the moment of birth. They are small replicas of their parents and are immediately able to hunt or, if plankton feeders, to swim through the water with their mouths slightly open so they can ingest minute animals.

Evidence that I have gathered and that is supported by the findings of other researchers confirms that embryonic sharks sometimes begin to feed *before* they are born, in some cases eating large numbers of their mother's undeveloped eggs, in others attacking and eating their own siblings. I first became aware of this precocious tendency when I was 12 years old while examining the internal organs of a newly killed female shark. I believe that she had been dead for about half an hour when I made a slit in the tissue of one of her wombs. I knew by its bulky shape that it was filled with embryos, so to prevent the tip of the knife from damaging the young, which I wanted to preserve in formalin, I introduced my left index into the cut and was almost immediately bitten on the knuckle. The resulting wound was half an inch long and deep enough to require stitches; its scar is still visible today. As matters turned out, seven of the twelve embryos were dead and three were close to dying; two were alive and so vigorous that I kept them in a tide pool for three months, until it was time to set them free in the Mediterranean at the end of the summer.

Since then, I have seen a number of cases of in-womb cannibalism, and although I have not been bitten by an embryo again, other researchers have shared my experience. It is to be presumed, however, that pup sharks do not attack their siblings or their mother's unfertilized eggs until they are nearing birth time. But this rather bizarre trait has not been recorded for any other kind of animal.

The majority of sharks that give birth to live young produce between six and twelve offspring, but some may have as many as four dozen at a time, the record to date being eighty-two for one tiger shark female. Gestation varies considerably between the species. Some pups are born within a few months, others take from one to two years to reach maturity.

One of the many puzzles surrounding selachians concerns the way in which a female's body deals with any of her embryos that may die before the time of birth. Unlike other multiple-birth animals, which in the majority of cases must abort all the young or probably die as a result of the massive infection caused by the decomposing fetus, dead shark embryos become mummified and are stillborn when their live siblings are ready to emerge! Equally puzzling, it has been established that when female sharks mate before their eggs are ready to be fertilized, the male's sperm is able to survive even after the death of the female.

How long does a typical shark live? Inasmuch as tests have shown that shark cells are capable of regeneration after death, the answer to this question may well be *forever* unless they are killed by predation, by the hand of man, by accident or by disease — if they ever *do* get sick.

To date, it is not possible to estimate the age of a shark, as can readily be done with bony fish, which have scales provided with annual growth rings. It can, however, be demonstrated by observation in captivity that selachians grow slowly, and it seems probable that they grow throughout their life-span, or at least well past the point when in other animals adulthood closes the ends of the bones and thereby forbids further development.

Similarly, it is not easy to find a relationship between the length and weight of a shark. I have tried many times to do so without any degree of success, as the following figures of length and weight, from one of my old notebooks, will show:

June 12/63: male tiger shark caught approximately six miles south of Fogio, Cape Verde Islands; length: 13' 2"; weight: 1,027 lbs.

June 16/63: male tiger shark, taken at about the same location as above; length: 12' 8"; weight: 453 lbs.

June 24/63: 15 miles west of Bissau, Portuguese Guinea; mako shark, male; length: 9' 5"; weight: 770 lbs. Same day, p.m.: mako, male; missing part of lower lobe of caudal fin and tip of dorsal; length: 10'; weight: 628 lbs.

These figures show that, in the first instance, a shark thirteen feet two inches long weighed 574 pounds more than another of the same species that was only six inches shorter. In the second case, the ten-foot mako was 142 pounds *lighter* than the second one, which was seven inches shorter. In *Shark Attack,* Dr. Baldridge reports an even more interesting comparison between two great white sharks, one of which was nine feet one inch long and weighed 750 pounds, while the other was exactly nine feet long but weighed only 280 pounds — a difference of 470 pounds for one inch of length! Obesity does not appear to be the answer, and neither is sickness, for such variations are too widespread and constant to be accounted for by either eventuality. I have invariably opened up captured sharks after weighing, so I know that the stomach contents, though quite variable, do not account for such large differences. In land animals, it is a rule of thumb that size equates the weight in healthy individuals, and it is for this reason that I find this shark peculiarity to be baffling.

Dr. Baldridge and his colleagues working on the U.S. Navy Shark Attack File came up with a series of figures for the Gulf Coast of Florida that were used to determine what they called the "Navy Standard Shark." After collecting 1,006 sharks over a period of nine years, they concluded that only 10 percent of selachians encountered in the area would be likely to exceed a length of ten feet and a weight of 440 pounds; but these figures were arrived at by feeding information into a computer and allotting percentile values to each individual or group. I have never put much faith in averages when these are applied to the affairs of nature, and I doubt that percentile values can mean a great deal when viewed realistically. Given the enormous element of chance involved in fishing — the angler does not know what is down there but only knows what he has caught — and the influences exerted on all animals of the same species by environmental conditions, these results should never be confused with biological reality.

Bony fish have swim bladders containing gas, by means of which they regulate their specific gravity to match the depth at which they are swimming. These bladders, or air sacs, located on the underside of the spine within the abdominal cavity, allow the fish to rise, sink or remain stationary at will and with hardly any effort. Sharks lack such a device, but their specific gravity is regulated by the amount of oil contained in their enormous livers, which may account for 20 to 25 percent of the total weight of a large selachian. By such means, the density of a shark is maintained at a point just a little heavier than that of seawater, or slightly lower than the point of negative buoyancy, allowing almost effortless movement through the water while conserving energy. But sharks cannot rise or dive without swimming, and if they stop, they sink slowly to the bottom.

Although the normal cruising rate of a shark is only about two miles an hour, it can move swiftly when it needs to. But it can only maintain maximum effort for a relatively short time. Nevertheless, because top speeds vary from species to species and even between individuals of the same kind, no firm figures can be given for all selachians. I have clocked sharks from the surface but never for more than one mile, and I had no means of knowing whether the individuals concerned were going flat out or not. However, I did record speeds of 14 knots (16 miles) for two bask-

ing sharks for three-quarters of a mile and found that they had no difficulty keeping ahead of my boat over that distance at that rate. But I
could not determine if they dived because they were tiring or simply
wanted to get away from me.

On another occasion, working a rubber boat powered by a 60-horse-
power outboard motor and going at full throttle, I was unable to keep up
with a tiger shark that was about 12 feet long. Later, testing the speed of
the boat along a measured course, I found that its maximum rate was 17
knots (19.55 miles).

Most sharks are cigar-shaped, or fusiform: their bodies taper toward
both ends from a maximum midpoint girth. In some, the body is gently
rounded; in others, the underside is relatively flat and the middle girth is
wide. The snouts are also variable, going from sharply pointed to rounded
and somewhat flattened. The hammerheads and bonnet sharks depart
radically from the above: the head of the former is shaped as its name
suggests and has no snout, and the latter looks rather like a spade.

A shark's tail, or caudal fin, is usually set vertically, so that it acts as a
rudder as well as an organ of propulsion. Most caudal fins are crescent-
shaped, but as a rule, the lower lobe of each is shorter than the upper,
which is notched about two-thirds of the way along the trailing edge; the
end of the spinal column branches upward from the body and enters the
upper lobe.

The majority of selachians have two dorsal fins: the first is the well-
known, sinister triangular organ so often seen when a shark is cruising
the surface; the second, which is usually small and hardly noticeable,
may serve no useful purpose. A few species have fairly large secondary
dorsals, and another group carries sharp spikes that jut out from the
leading edges of both fins — armament that is presumably used for
defense. Others, such as the thresher and the six-gill, have only one dorsal, which is set closer to the tail.

On the underside of the body are three pairs of fins. Starting from
the tail end, these are: anal, pelvic and pectoral. In males, the pelvic fins
have been modified to form twin sexual organs called claspers, which are
used to transfer sperm into the female's reproductive tract. The pectoral

fins in all species of sharks are somewhat saber-shaped — they are wide
where they are joined to the body and taper to a point. They are usually
long, but because of the way in which they are attached, they cannot be
rotated and are only capable of up-and-down movement. The fins of
most bony fish, in contrast, are narrow and flexible where they join the
body, wide at the distal ends and carried at a vertical or near vertical
angle. These things allow a fish to slow down or stop and back up, but
sharks, unable to rotate their pectorals so as to use them as brakes, can
only halt by stilling the sweeping motion of their tails. They cannot go
into reverse and must steer themselves off course if they are about to col-
lide with an obstruction or another shark; or, if they make a pass at a victim and miss, they must then swing wide for a second pass, much as an
aircraft must do if it is not perfectly aligned with the runway.

Sharks control their balance and direction by combining the uses of
their tails and their dorsal and pectoral fins; their low density allows
them to move easily through the water at any given depth and to swim
along a straight course with a minimum of effort. Because the large pectoral fins are positioned forward of a shark's center of gravity, they tend
to push the body upward, but the flexible lower lobe of the tail creates a
downward thrust and thus counterbalances the lift. Meanwhile, the large
dorsal fin keeps the body upright, acting rather like the keel of a sailboat
but in reverse order. By altering the angle of the pectorals and accelerat-
ing or slowing the beat of the tail, a shark can go up or down as it swims
along a direct course, its hydrodynamically engineered shape sliding
almost silently through the waters, its movement sometimes snakelike
because, as it wags the last third of its body to generate propulsion, it
often turns the first third in the opposite direction so as to increase its
angle of vision. When swimming slowly in this way, the serpentine
motion becomes more pronounced, and as the hard muscles bunch and
relax, the skin forms corrugations that seem to travel in opposite directions.

To breathe, a shark must cause water to continuously pass over its
gills, special organs that are the equivalent of terrestrial lungs, which are
well supplied with blood vessels. These absorb oxygen from the water

and release carbon dioxide from the blood. Although a minority of sharks are able to pump water over their gills while lying stationary on the bottom, most of them must keep on the move, mouths slightly open, to allow the sea to wash over the gills and to escape through gill slits, five to seven of which, according to species, are located on each side of the body just ahead of the pectoral fins. Behind each eye, sharks and rays have an opening, the spiracle, that is connected to the gill chambers and through which water also passes to aid in breathing. Spiracles are ancestral gill slits, modified to their present shape and function so as to make room for the development of jaws.

It is widely believed that sharks must keep moving continuously in order to stay alive. This is not so; they can and do rest, sometimes by allowing themselves to slowly drift downward, on other occasions by lying on the bottom. Those species that cannot pump water over their gills while at a standstill can hold their breath for at least half an hour — many a shark fisherman has had a nasty surprise when a supposedly lifeless selachian suddenly revived on board the boat. More than a few people have been hurt, some mortally, by such "dead" fish.

The majority of vertebrates have teeth, but a hunting shark does much better than that, its entire body being one huge mouth! Within its elastic jaws are the formidable teeth that serve to seize and kill prey and are also capable of cutting off great scoops of meat from even the largest animals, or of slicing through tissue, sinew and bone to literally chop up the prey. The first row of teeth in each jaw contains the functional weapons. Behind them are a number of reserve rows, the most forward of which is almost fully developed, waiting to replace any that are lost during attack (a process that takes about a week), the last row containing tooth buds. All lie flat inside the mouth when this is closed, each overlapping the other, points toward the back. When the mouth opens, the functional teeth become erect.

Quite often a shark appears to have more than one leading row of teeth, but although there are extra dentures to be seen, the rearmost are scattered untidily along the gums, having moved up prematurely from the first reserve crescent. This gives the mouth an even more fearsome aspect and is quite common in great whites and tigers.

Each species has its own special teeth, a characteristic that has often helped identify unseen human attackers when entire teeth, or their broken points, have been found embedded in the victim's bones. Teeth are lost rather easily because they are not securely anchored in jawbone, as in most other vertebrates. They also break readily because they are usually thin and brittle, although their hardness rates on the Mohs' scale match that of steel. As a rule, those in the upper jaw are triangular and sharp-pointed and have fine, sometimes serrated, cutting edges, while those contained in the lower jaw tend to be spikelike and are used to hold the prey while the upper, cutting teeth are brought into action split seconds after contact.

Instead of the scales that protect and streamline the bodies of bony fish, shark skin is covered in tiny teeth, or denticles, as they are called. Although they are much smaller, these toothlets have the same structure as the teeth in a shark's mouth. In some species, the denticles are rounded and smooth, which makes their owners look as though they are covered in glass beads; in others, they are pointed and backward curving; and in yet others, they are sharp and straight.

Those sharks that are covered in sharp denticles — and most are — have developed taste buds on their bodies — little pits in the skin that lie between two denticles which can distinguish between edible and inedible substances. The heaviest concentration of these sensorial crypts, to give them their proper name, are found forward of the pectorals. When a shark rubs up against an object, the toothlets scrape particles from it, much as sandpaper removes dust from a piece of wood. Friction and pressure push these samples into the sensorial crypts, where they are tasted, and the results are instantly registered.

Because the jaws are set on the underside of the body and are far back from the snout, it was once generally thought that these fish had to turn on their sides, or even on their backs, in order to bite, a view that is still common today. This is not so. Sharks can bite from any angle because their jaws are double-hinged.

By raising its nose as it opens its mouth, a shark causes its upper teeth to project forward, a circumstance that allows for considerable attack flexibility. Indeed, some dangerous sharks can project their upper teeth to such an extent that they can slash with them, much as one might do with a saber. Sharks use this tactic when they fight among themselves, and it has also been used during human attacks. These raking cuts do much damage.

On occasion, sharks have been known to use their noses during the preliminaries of an attack, sometimes hitting a surface target with such force that it is thrust right out of the water. A number of people have been hit in this way, in some cases so forcefully that witnesses have said the victims looked as though they were standing on water for a fraction of time. Similarly, the fins of a large shark, although perhaps not intentionally used as weapons, are capable of inflicting serious injuries if a person is struck by them, for the edges of all fins are also covered by dermal teeth and can rip through flesh as easily as a serrated knife cuts a slice of bread.

Apart from their formidable array of weapons, sharks have developed highly specialized and acute sensory organs that are used for location of prey and for purposes of navigation. Running along both sides of their bodies are lateral lines that are sensitive to pressure changes and to vibrations and are remarkably similar to man's sonar equipment. All fish have these lines, but sharks have developed them to fine pitch. Starting at the root of the spinal column, they travel along both flanks before branching around the eyes, nostrils and mouth. Technically, the laterals are called phonoreceptors and are structured rather like small canals, filled with water or a jellylike substance and connected to the outside surface of the skin by numerous pores. Embedded on the underside of each canal is a main nerve that is connected by a series of branches to an equal number of receptor cells. The material that fills the canals is highly sensitive to the movement of environmental water and produces impulses that reach the sensorial cells. These, in turn, communicate sensation to the trunk nerve and through it to a shark's brain.

On the head and nose of sharks are openings known as Lorenzini flasks. These enable selachians to detect minute electrical fields. Such amazing sensitivity is the highest discovered in any animal.

Sharks have an acute sense of smell and can detect from considerable distances even the tiniest odor-bearing particles present in the water. Their nostrils, strangely shaped and resembling a horizontal or leaning S, contain membranes known as Schneider folds that increase the olfactory surfaces. Water constantly flows through these folds, bringing with it scent particles. When these are haphazard, emanating from bits and pieces of organic flotsam, a shark's interest is not roused; but when a steady odor stream is detected, a hungry selachian will follow it to its distant source as unerringly as a good hound follows a fresh trail.

Although the eyes of sharks are unable to bring objects into sharp focus and therefore they cannot distinguish detail as clearly as most mammals, they are extremely sensitive to movement and general form, even in the poorest light. But whether these fish can perceive color as we know it is a question still being debated in some scientific circles. Nonetheless, it is a fact that all primary colors reflect light and therefore produce different levels of brightness, of tones that contrast with their background and of shading — all of which are easily detectable by selachians.

The eyes of man and those of a few other animals accommodate for distance by changing the curvature of their lenses, but sharks, like conventional fish and amphibians, focus by moving their lenses forward and backward, in the same way that a camera is focused.

This arrangement may not be as efficient as our own and may account for the inability of selachians to bring objects into sharp relief. On the other hand, a system of shutters located behind each retina allows sharks to see at depths that are only marginally lighter than total darkness. These little blinds, or tapetum, are silvered in front, and during conditions of poor visibility, they return light by reflection after it has passed through the retina, in this way twice utilizing the same amount of light absorbed by the eyes. In bright surface conditions, the tapetum become coated by cells that contain black pigment, which migrate along each little blind and cover it entirely, acting rather like very dark sunglasses and neutralizing the mirror surface of the plates.

Apart from the obvious advantages of this system for an animal that spends most of its time in penumbral conditions, it also compensates for the fact that a shark has no eyelids as such. Instead, its eyes are shielded from abrasive substances by a nictitating membrane that blinks upward from its source under each eye. This transparent fold of skin also occurs in amphibians, reptiles, birds and some mammals.

Apart from feeling vibrations given off by oceanic sounds, selachians can hear quite well and over long distances, despite the fact that they do not have external ear openings. This is because sound travels through water at about 5,000 feet per second and does so more easily than it can through the terrestrial atmosphere. (Through air, it travels at only about 1,100 feet per second.)

The internal or visceral organs of a shark are arranged loosely inside its body and are supported *outside* the thin abdominal skin by the water in which it swims, rather than by muscular or ligamental attachments. Because of this, the viscera tear easily when the animal is pulled out of the water, for the organs flop downward if it is lifted by the head, or spread unnaturally if the fish lies on the unyielding deck of a boat. This arrangement of intestines is probably a shark's only anatomical weakness, and even this is of no great consequence when it is in the water. Nevertheless, dolphins and porpoises have found this flaw and can kill large sharks by repeatedly butting them in the stomach with their hard beaks, sometimes hitting so violently that a victim is tossed right out of the water, its internal organs ruptured.

The esophagus of a shark is large, allowing it to swallow enormous pieces of meat. Its correspondingly big stomach is somewhat cone-shaped and ends in a surprisingly short intestine: about eight feet long in a ten-foot shark as compared to some thirty-one feet in an adult man of average stature. Within this folded inner tube, on the underside, is an organ called the spiral valve that consists of intricately folded mucous membranes that provide more surface area for the absorption of nourishment, making up for the shortness of the main intestine.

Selachians digest their food in much the same way that other animals do, yet they can retain portions of a meal intact and in a good state of preservation for extended periods of time. How they do this is so far unknown. Additionally, sharks can ingest anything at all, edible or not, a habit in which they frequently indulge. When they have swallowed too much junk, they simply throw up the lot.

The brain of a shark has been greatly underestimated by many observers, some of whom have gone so far as to claim that this organ is little more than a primitive bundle of sensory ganglia incapable of making calculated decisions. But scientists have demonstrated that the ratio of brain-to-body weight of selachians is similar to that of many mammals and birds — man and other primates excepted. And in recent times, investigators, myself included, have established beyond a doubt that sharks learn from experience, have a memory that retains information for a long time and can distinguish between those environmental influences that are rewarding or dangerous and those that offer neither profit nor threat.

Viewed from the top, facing front, a shark's brain looks somewhat like the ornate handle of a dagger, the hilt of which would represent the *medulla oblongate*, the most posterior part of the vertebrate brain that merges with the spinal cord. This coordinates impulses received from the lateral lines, the ears and the taste and touch receptors. It also contains vital centers that regulate breathing movements, the blood vessels, the heart and other important reflexes. Next is the cerebellum that, among other things, controls and coordinates muscular movements and balance. Encountered in ascending order are paired optic lobes, in which visual sensations are received; these are quite small, supporting the evidence that sharks are somewhat myopic. Ahead of the optic centers lie well-developed cerebral hemispheres. Lastly, at the front of the brain are the large olfactory lobes that give these fish such an acute sense of smell.

The cerebral hemispheres have been presumed to deal mainly with the coordination of scent stimuli. Yet this is too facile an explanation to account for such a complex part of the forebrain, especially in view of the fact that the enormous cortex found in our own species, which gave us the ability to reason, developed as an outgrowth of the cerebral hemispheres. Having observed many sharks in a variety of places for long periods of time, I know that these animals are able to reason; and although such intellectualizing is limited compared to our own, it does exist. Its source, therefore, must be found within the hemispheres.

For centuries, some western technologists have felt themselves to be superior to the laws of nature. For this reason, it seems to me they have felt threatened by natural forces they were unable to understand, forces beyond their manipulative control. Unlike societies whose beliefs and religions were nature-oriented and united them with the entire spectrum of life, some westerners have clung to their credo of superiority, refusing to accept that other sentient forms can think and feel and are better able to survive within their own habitats.

Constrained by such dogma, we have arbitrarily divided the world of nature, classifying as "good" those things we believe can give us profit, and as "bad" those in which we see no benefit or which we deem to be harmful. Such black-and-white thinking has encouraged us to declare our persons sacred, so that when we discover an animal capable of harming us, we become outraged (yet we have accepted with strange equanimity the countless killings and devastations caused by our multiple wars).

When a powerful and potentially dangerous animal appears to have intellectual capacity, it is doubly feared. Many people refuse to believe that real intelligence can exist in any but the human species.

Men would like to believe that sharks are not capable of planning an attack. It may well be for this reason that we have not engaged in any real studies of the intellectual capabilities of these fish until recent times.

Not long ago, discussing intelligence with a number of animal behaviorists, I voiced opposition to IQ testing in controlled conditions because we then seek to measure mental capacity out of context with a subject's habitat. The mark of intelligence, I argued, is denoted by an animal's ability to live successfully within its own environment. I still believe this. That is why I consider sharks to be intelligent, for they surely live successfully in the realm that they inhabit.

# ABOUT THE AUTHOR

Born at sea in Spanish territorial waters and educated in England, R.D. Lawrence is an inveterate adventurer, biologist and wildlife researcher with a rare love of animals. He is the author of 25 books on wildlife and ecology, including *The North Runner,* the story of an unusual wolf-dog; *Secret Go the Wolves,* about Lawrence's experiences raising two wolf cubs; *The Zoo That Never Was,* in which he describes some of the animals he has cared for; *Voyage of the Stella,* an account of a solitary six-month exploration of the coasts of British Columbia; *Canada's National Parks;* and *The Ghost Walker.* When not in the wilderness, Lawrence lives in Ontario's Haliburton Highlands.

# INDEX